PSYCHOGENESIS

PSYCHOGENESIS
The Early Development of
Gender Identity

Elizabeth R. Moberly

ROUTLEDGE & KEGAN PAUL LIMITED
London, Boston, Melbourne and Henley

First published in 1983
by Routledge & Kegan Paul Ltd
39 Store Street, London WC1E 7DD,
9 Park Street, Boston, Mass. 02108, USA,
296 Beaconsfield Parade, Middle Park,
Melbourne, 3206, Australia, and
Broadway House, Newtown Road,
Henley-on-Thames, Oxon RG9 1EN
Printed in Great Britain by
Billing & Sons Ltd, Worcester ·

Library of Congress Cataloging in Publication Data

Moberly, Elizabeth R.
Psychogenesis, the early development of gender identity.
Bibliography: p.
Includes index.
1. Homosexuality. 2. Change of sex. 3. Identity
(Psychology) I. Title. [DNLM: 1. Identification
(Psychology) BF 692.2 M687p]
RC558.M6 1982   155.3   82-16526

ISBN 0-7100-9271-7

CONTENTS

PREFACE

This study represents the fruit of seven years' work in gender identity research. It is based solely on the existing psycho-analytic data available in this area, which I believe to have been insufficiently assessed hitherto. In making this extensive theoretical revision, my concern has been to provide a more thorough elucidation of the implications of these data, and to suggest a fresh perspective on their import.

I am grateful to Lucy Cavendish College, Cambridge, for the award of Guest Membership while I wrote this book; to numerous specialist libraries in Oxford and Cambridge, at which I worked; to Dr Farrell Toombs of Toronto, for assistance with some working expenses; and to my friends, whose support and prayers made all the difference to the progress of this study. The responsibility for the opinions here expressed must, of course, rest with the author alone.

Elizabeth R. Moberly

Cambridge 1979

INTRODUCTION

In the discussion that follows, I consider both homosexuality and transsexualism from a psychodynamic point of view. Transsexualism has been one of the least explored areas of the human personality. The most prominent current hypothesis suggests that the male-to-female transsexual acquires a gender identity through a non-conflictual process of learning (Stoller, 1975). By contrast, I have suggested that transsexualism in both genders has a similar aetiology, and that the condition stems from unresolved childhood trauma. Radical disidentification from the parent of the same sex results in a psychodynamic structure of same-sex ambivalence: there is a defensive detachment from the same-sex love-source and a reparative striving for a restored attachment. This same dynamic is involved in homosexuality, but in varying degree. At one extreme there is little to distinguish homosexuality from transsexualism, in that both are based on radical disidentification, whether or not this manifests itself in the form of an apparent cross-gender awareness. More commonly, homosexuality is marked by a lesser degree of same-sex ambivalence. However, the essential dynamic is the same in all cases, and thus the difference between these conditions is one of degree rather than of kind. The defensive detachment from the same-sex love-source implies that the process of same-sex identification is still to some extent incomplete, whether radically or only partially so. On this understanding, homosexuality itself becomes a problem of gender identity.

Freud's well-known hypothesis of a link between homosexuality and paranoia (the Schreber case, 1911) is examined in some detail. Paranoia is regarded as an extreme form of defensive detachment from a love-source - a detachment based on a pathological 'mourning' reaction to childhood trauma. The love-source may happen to be the parent of the same sex or, equally, the parent of the opposite sex. In the former case, the condition is that known as homosexual paranoia; in the latter, there is genuinely heterosexual paranoia. Freud's hypothesis is considered to be both verified and qualified. There is a significant link between homosexuality and paranoia, but not all paranoia is homosexual; and, just as importantly, not all homosexuality is paranoid.

Homosexuality and transsexualism alike imply a defect in the capacity for relating to the same sex - not the opposite sex, as is commonly assumed. The capacity for same-sex love marks

only one side of the overall phenomenon of same-sex ambivalence.
What is pathological about this is the defensive detachment from
the love-source, and the missing growth consequent on this.
Needs for love, dependency and identification which are normally
met through the medium of an attachment to a (parental) love-
source of the same sex, have remained unmet. The capacity for
same-sex love is the attempt to restore this disrupted attachment and hence to make up for missing growth. The homosexual
response is itself the reparative drive towards restoration, i.e.
it is not itself the problem, but rather the attempted solution to
the problem. However, the capacity for same-sex love is not
essentially sexual, even if it frequently undergoes secondary
eroticisation.

Heterosexuality is the goal of human development, but it
implies a heteropsychologic personality structure, which is based
on the fulfilment of homo-emotional needs and not their abrogation. Homosexuality is not the goal, but it is the means to the
goal and the goal cannot be truly achieved without the meeting
of these needs. Therapy should aim at undoing the defensive
detachment from the same-sex love-source, and at bringing the
reparative drive to its fulfilment.

Research hitherto has given relatively little attention to the
lesbian and the female-to-male transsexual, and I have attempted
to rectify this imbalance, though at the same time without
neglecting their male and male-to-female counterparts.

In what is already a wide-ranging and detailed study, I have
felt unable to include more than a brief mention of the condition
of transvestism. However, my reflections on homosexuality and
transsexualism may perhaps suggest avenues for exploration
which other workers in this field may care to take up. It should
be noted that this study does not discuss physiological inter-
sexuality (hermaphroditism), as distinct from transsexualism.

My aim in this study has been to find and to apply a hypothesis
that has internal coherence, consistency with the known facts,
and an ability to illuminate hitherto little-understood phenomena.
The results of this quest are now offered for general appraisal.

1 THE SCHREBER CASE AND THE QUEST FOR HISTORICAL REALITY

One of the most fascinating cases in psychoanalytic literature is that of Daniel Paul Schreber (1842-1911), a judge of the German high court who spent many of his later years under psychiatric care on a diagnosis of paranoia. In 1903, between his second and third periods of hospitalisation, he wrote a detailed account of his experiences entitled 'Memoirs of My Nervous Illness'. On a traditional psychiatric understanding, these provide abundant evidence of delusions of persecution and hallucinations. Rays; divine 'miracles' involving – for instance – a sense of heat or cold or compression; and – most particularly – 'soul murder', attributed in turn to Schreber's physician, Dr Flechsig, and to God; all these are, at first sight, standard psychotic material, involving a break with reality and the irruption of pathological intrapsychic contents. There has, however, been a singularly interesting line of interpretation of the Schreber case, which has attempted to correlate this 'psychotic' material with Schreber's childhood experiences. To the extent that such a correlation is valid, this would call into question the standard assessment of paranoid delusions and hallucinations as merely imaginary. If some genuine memory contributed to their origin, to that extent they must be seen as realistic. This does not, of itself, suggest that the experiences hitherto denoted as delusions and hallucinations are entirely justifiable, and in no way unrealistic. Such an assessment would not be justified solely on the grounds of the proposed correlation with early memories. Howver, the value of such a correlation should be considerable. Hence we shall attempt here to trace the quest for historical reality in the condition known as paranoia.

In 1911, the year of Schreber's death, Sigmund Freud wrote his formative account of the Schreber case, based on the text of Schreber's 'Memoirs'. Since he did not make use of any other material, such as the published works of Schreber's father, it was not open to him to draw any kind of correlation between the 'Memoirs' and other data. Freud did, however, comment somewhat prophetically:[1]

> It remains for the future to decide whether . . . there is more truth in Schreber's delusion than other people are as yet prepared to believe.

Freud did not himself develop this line of thought any further, at any rate as regards the actual case of Schreber. However, he did suggest the theoretical basis for such a development in one of the writings of his later years, 'Constructions in analysis' (1937a). Here he states:[2]

> Perhaps it may be a general characteristic of hallucinations to which sufficient attention has not hitherto been paid that in them something that has been experienced in infancy and then forgotten returns . . . something that the child has seen or heard at a time when he could still hardly speak and that now forces its way into consciousness, probably distorted and displaced owing to the operation of forces that are opposed to this return.

Freud does not doubt that a distortion of present reality is involved. He sees the therapeutic task as one of[3]

> liberating the fragment of historical truth from its distortions and its attachments to the actual present day and in leading it back to the point in the past to which it belongs.

This proposition of 'a fragment of historical truth' is crucial for subsequent developments. Unfortunately, it was some years before Freud's suggestion was taken up. Waelder (1951) refers to Freud's idea that it is this element of truth in them that accounts for delusional ideas being held so tenaciously. He speaks of 'a return of the disclaimed in distorted form'. However, Waelder's discussion treats only of the paranoid's intrapsychic conflict, and he makes no attempt to consider the actual circumstances of Schreber's childhood, wherein this 'element of truth' is supposed to have originated.

In 1956 Baumeyer provided additional data for consideration in the Schreber case. Shifting the focus from Schreber himself, he sheds light on the character of his parents. His mother was nervous and prone to rapid changes of mood. And his father suffered from obsessional ideas with homicidal tendencies. These facts, gleaned from the case-records of Schreber's asylum, are noteworthy, and of themselves suggest a reason for further investigating Schreber's family environment. Baumeyer adds, on the evidence of Schreber's married sister, that Schreber's life was 'almost entirely under the influence of the overpowering father figure'.

Freud's clue of the importance of historical truth was at last taken up by Niederland (1959), whose paper is crucial to the line of development here considered. Taking Freud's suggestion as his starting-point, Niederland scrutinises the character of Schreber's father and the nature of his relationship with his children, in the hope of ascertaining what the father may have contributed to the son's psychopathology. Dr Schreber (i.e. Schreber's father) was a well-known and much-published physician and pedagogue. His numerous writings provide important evidence for consideration in the Schreber case - evidence that Freud did not take into account, although it had been available in print for half a century and more before he wrote his study of Schreber.

Dr Schreber believed in the strict and well-regimented upbringing of children, and the methods he detailed in his writings were applied within his own family, ostensibly to further their health and welfare. Upon investigation, there prove to be notable similarities between the 'miracles' detailed in Schreber's 'Memoirs' i.e. the supposedly delusional reflections of a middle-aged man, and the actual disciplinary devices and exercises experienced by Schreber as a growing boy, at his father's instigation. A 'compression-of-the-chest miracle' recalls the iron cross bar Dr Schreber used to force children to sit up correctly. The 'head-compressing machine' recalls a device worn to hold the head straight. 'Miracles of cold' are suggestive of the compulsory cold baths that were part of the routine of the Schreber household. 'Miracles' affecting the opening and closing of the eyes recall the eye exercises detailed by Dr Schreber. The possibility of correlation suggests itself repeatedly and in some detail, as can be seen by comparing the writings of Schreber and his father, and hence the cumulative weight of the evidence tends to suggest that this correlation is in some sense significant. In what precise sense it is significant is another matter, and has remained open to debate.

Without listing these correlations in detail, Niederland insists on their central importance. He notes:

> A comparison of the paternal and filial texts makes it difficult, at times, to know exactly where the father's medical mythology ends and the son's delusional mythology begins.

Again,

> We will . . . encounter certain psychic derivatives of these experiences as components of some of the 'miracled-up' delusional formations which fill the pages of the *Memoirs*.

And, to press home the point,

> It reads like a highly condensed, symbolized, archaically distorted, yet essentially correct version of many of the paternal physical maneuvres to which the young Schreber was subjected.

While noting the importance of genuine memory-traces, it is equally clear that Niederland has no doubt that such memories have become distorted and are at variance with contemporary reality. Whatever may have been contributed by historical truth to Schreber's ideas, they have also been subject to a pathological development, under the influence of instinctual drives, libidinal

conflicts, introjective-projective mechanisms, and processes of
regression and restitution. Niederland's findings do not, on his
own conclusions, essentially disturb the Freudian analysis of the
Schreber case.

Over a decade later, Niederland's findings were taken up and
reassessed by Schatzman (1972, 1973). The latter infers that a
finding of genuine persecutory experiences is incompatible with
a diagnosis of paranoia, in which - by definition - the sense of
persecution is illusory.[4]

To call (such persons) paranoid, which presupposes they
are not really persecuted, but imagine it, is false and misleading.

And,[5]

What is clinically called paranoia is often the partial realization
- as through a glass darkly - that one has been or is persecuted.

To invalidate a person's sense of persecution is quite improper.
The correct therapeutic step is to investigate the social context,
in order to ascertain the origin of these feelings. The assumption
is that the sense of being persecuted is an accurate response
to the actual behaviour of other people.

Niederland and Schatzman agree in seeing undeniable correlations between Schreber's childhood experiences and his later
reflections. They differ radically in their understanding of what
conclusions may legitimately be drawn from these correlations.
In effect, Niederland draws no further conclusions: memory-
traces are merely an additional datum contributing to the subsequent psychopathology. Schatzman, by contrast, sees the
historicity of persecutory experiences as tantamount to the
denial of any psychopathology. If you have genuinely been
persecuted, you may not be denoted 'paranoid', in that this
would be a self-contradictory statement. Schatzman does have
a point here, since the actual definition of paranoia has never
been revised. Despite Freud's suggestion (1937a) of genuine
memory-traces in psychotic material, and Niederland's confirmation of this in the Schreber case (1959), paranoid ideas have
generally continued to be regarded as altogether illusory. Thus,
if one has experienced persecution, it is certainly improper to
apply a concept that denies that this is so. To this extent one
may agree with Schatzman. However, if one were to revise the
definition of paranoia to allow for the possibility of its partial
historicity, much of the force would be removed from Schatzman's
argument. Moreover, it would no longer be contradictory to
assert that a persecuted person may be genuinely paranoid,
since the assertion of partial truth implies that partial untruth
is also involved. Paranoia is, on our understanding, neither
totally illusory nor totally non-illusory, but combines elements

of both truth and falsehood. More specifically, what it would seem to involve is a mixture of past truth and present untruth.

The actual experiences of Schreber's childhood are given facts. Their correlation with Schreber's later writings is well argued and highly plausible. But to what extent may authentic experience of the past have unfairly affected the understanding of the present? On what grounds may one either argue for, or rule out, the possibility of subsequent distortion? Niederland's discussion of Schreber suggests that Schreber's later reflections were true to the past. But Niederland does not give grounds for suggesting that Schreber's ideas were true to the present. This is the crucial point. If a sense of persecution can be justified entirely by present facts alone, there is no ground for the use of the term 'paranoia'. But if a sense of persecution is not justified by present facts, or only partially justified by them, then something is amiss. Whether or not the feeling of being persecuted may be legitimately referred to past events, the vital point is that to a greater or lesser extent there has been a loss of contact with present reality. It is this discrepancy between past and present that must be accounted for. Schatzman does not do justice to this point, and hence his attempt to draw out the significance of Niederland's data must be considered unsatisfactory in this fundamental respect. One may agree with Schatzman that feelings of persecution may at least sometimes be referred to actual events in the individual's social environment. However, this only informs us that it is important to distinguish between realistic and unrealistic feelings of persecution. Once the distinction is drawn, there is no discussion of unrealistic feelings and their significance. Schatzman's work is helpful in insisting on the significance of the reality factor - which may not have been sufficiently appreciated hitherto - but is otherwise one-sided.

The combination of past reality with present unreality would seem to be especially clear in the Schreber case. However accurate his thoughts may be as memories of the past, however true to the experience of his childhood, they are not an accurate representation of present reality. For this reason, Schatzman's dichotomy of either paranoia or persecution is false to the available data. We may suggest that the present state of the question may more accurately be stated thus: How does genuine persecution, in the early history of the individual, lead to genuine paranoia, i.e. to a greater or lesser distortion of subsequent reality?

In this connection, it will be of value to comment specifically on the significance of the reality factor, since in practice it has tended to be either underestimated (by many psychiatrists) or overestimated (by Schatzman, as here criticised). What the evidence suggests is that the reality factor is (a) existent, not absent; (b) partial, not entire; (c) linked to the past, to the extent of involving some discrepancy with the present. Adding up these points as here spelled out, we may suggest as a con-

clusion that the so-called delusional contents of the paranoid
state are not imaginary, but are anachronistic. It is this
anachronism that remains as yet unaccounted for, and that
justifies the assumption of some form of pathological development.
We are still faced with the need to explain why certain experiences of the past should in some way result in a break with
present reality.

Turning aside from delusional contents in general, we shall
focus on the sense of persecution in particular. Schreber's
sense of persecution at the hands of a father-figure would seem
accurate as related to his actual childhood experiences. But the
projection of this feeling on to his physician, Dr Flechsig, and
on to God, does not seem justified. We are to contrast what, on
the given evidence, seems an accurate assessment of the childhood relationship with an inaccurate evaluation of adult relationships, based on the unjustified correlation of one with the other.
It is the relationship on which the sense of persecution is
focused, and in which we find both past reality and present
distortion. It is the relationship upon which both the genuine
persecution and the genuine pathology are focused.

One may take as one's starting-point the given situation of
reality, that is, the genuinely persecutory experiences that are
to be found in Schreber's early history. At this point it would
seem that 'inner reality' and 'outer reality' coincided. If the
young Schreber felt 'persecuted', it was because his father was
behaving towards him in a 'persecutory' manner, i.e. with rigid
and all-controlling strictness, as there is abundant evidence to
suggest. In later life we find Schreber's ability to relate to
father-figures, viz. his physician and God, is affected so as to
involve a distortion of contemporary reality. But what the
distortion involves is in fact an accurate, if symbolised, reproduction of the experiences of Schreber's early years. This would
suggest that we may find it significant to link early social interaction, viz. the parent-child relationship, with the child's actual
capacity for relationship. The former would seem to have
affected the latter, to the extent of permanently damaging the
child's ability to relate to father-figures. What the evidence
would seem to suggest is that the young Schreber internalised
the effects of the difficult relationship with his father; and
that these traumatic effects remained unresolved into adult life,
where they were capable of being reproduced without modification. However, what this would imply is that the basic
mechanism involved in paranoia, at least in the Schreber case,
is not projection, but transference.

Schreber's 'psychotic' ideas replicate a genuine interpersonal
situation of the past, i.e. they once had an accurate contact
with external reality. Their reproduction in later life may be
termed projection only in so far as the phenomenon known as
transference uses the mechanism of projecting early reality on
to a contemporary situation. However, this is not projection in
the usual, more narrowly defined sense, of imposing material

that is merely intrapsychic on to external reality. What is
happening is that early social reality is being 'projected' on to
contemporary social reality. And this may most accurately be
described as a transference situation.

We have thus two referents for our process of investigation:
Schreber's childhood, where reality is not yet distorted; and
his adult life, where there is a departure from present reality
involved precisely by his fidelity to past reality. We may attempt
to ascertain the effect of his childhood on his capacity for
relationship from both of these referents. On the one hand,
from considering the likely effect of known facts, in childhood.
On the other hand, from considering the nature of his subsequent relational capacity, which is considered to have been
distorted by effects carried over from the past. By retrospec-
tive correlation, one may attempt to reconstruct the shape of
the trauma suffered in childhood through considering the
distortion in the analogous relationship in adult life, i.e. from
considering the nature of the transference.

One constant factor would seem to be the sense of persecution
vis-à-vis a father-figure, accurate to the reality of early life
and internalised and reproduced in later life. In later life this
sense of persecution is found in conjunction with a sense of
needing to love and be loved by the persecutory figure. These
two aspects, of both hate and love vis-à-vis the self-same
figure, are linked in the situation of adult life, where at any
rate the emotion of hate is regarded as part of the transference
from the early social situation. What of the parallel aspect of
the need for love? Could this too be part of the transference,
i.e. to be linked with the reality of early events? We may
suggest a hypothesis.

Persecutory experience in childhood leads not only to hatred,
on account of persecution; but also blocks the child's capacity
to receive love from the person who is acting in a persecutory
manner. The parent is supposed to be the normal love-source
in the child's process of growth, and for most people it would
seem that this process takes place more or less satisfactorily.
But if the love-source behaves persecutorily, is it not plausible
that the process may be blocked? The child may not be able to
receive the love that is normally received from the love-source.
This normal need is, abnormally, left unmet. Suppose, then,
that this unmet need to love and be loved is also repressed
and carried over into adult life, just as is the sense of persecution. On this hypothesis, one would expect to find in adult
life a twofold phenomenon of need for love and hatred for the
love-source, which is seen as persecutory. This is precisely
the so-called 'paranoid' phenomenon, and at the same time is a
hypothesis that would make sense of the known events of childhood in this particular case history. Our hypothesis is that the
paranoid phenomenon is a twofold internalisation of the effects
of a traumatic relationship in childhood, which persists unmodi-
fied and with the capacity for replication in later life. Persecutory

behaviour would seem not only to have had a traumatic effect
on the libidinal bond in childhood but, more seriously, to have
affected the subsequent libidinal capacity of the growing
individual.

In connection with this hypothesis, it should be noted that
the emotions involved in paranoia, love and hate alike, are considered to have been originally grounded in social reality, and
to have been a response to actual behaviour by some other
person. This twofold response would have been both accurate
to the facts of the early situation, and readily comprehensible,
as a consequence of experiencing persecutory behaviour.
Hitherto, the characteristically paranoid feelings of love and
hate have been assumed to be merely intrapsychic, and not to
be in any way correlated with external reality. We here suggest
that what is involved is the replication of early social reality
with its abiding traumatic effects. The reality factor applies,
in their origin, to the feelings both of hate and of the need for
love. This point is of particular importance. The clue of an
element of historical truth in psychosis has never been adequately followed up. Often it has not been followed up at all.
And, where it has been followed up, the attempt has not been
made to correlate it with possible effects on the child's actual
libidinal capacity; or, in connection with this, to make the
further correlation of linking these effects with the typically
'paranoid' emotions to be found in later life during a period of
overt psychosis.

Freud's well-known analysis of the emotions of love and hate
in the paranoid is an entirely intrapsychic construct.[6] It makes
no attempt at correlation with the early interpersonal situation,
and indeed assumes that no such correlation can be made. It
runs as follows: The emotion of love, 'I (a man) love him (a man)',
is denied: 'No, I do not love him, I hate him.' The paranoid
then projects his own emotion of hate on to the person whom he
has denied loving: 'He hates me.' Thus, the hatred of the
former love-object is taken as justifying the paranoid's own
hatred of him: 'I hate him, *because* he persecutes me.' The
psychological mechanisms of denial and projection are fundamental to this construct. If, however, the paranoid phenomenon
is essentially one of *transference,* these mechanisms become
redundant. The contrasting emotions may be linked with the
actual facts of the early interpersonal situation. We may rewrite
the construct as follows:

> I [a small boy] need to love and receive love from him [my
> father]. However, he [my father] is behaving persecutorily
> to me. Therefore, I hate him, on account of his hateful
> behaviour. Likewise, my need to love and receive love from
> him is blocked, because he - the love-source - is behaving
> so hatefully.

Freud commented that 'observation leaves room for no doubt

that the persecutor is some one who was once loved.[17] We would
here suggest that this statement has far more truth in it than
Freud ever gave it credit for. It is not, as he thought, a description of libidinal conflict isolated from external referents.
Rather, it is the accurate assessment of a traumatic interpersonal
situation in early life, which has been internalised with the
potential for subsequent replication. Actual persecutory behaviour accounts both for the emotion of hate and for the need
for love which - blocked by the hateful behaviour of the love-
source - has been left unmet, and thus has persisted into
adult life as a need yet to be met.

This hypothesis has the advantages of internal consistency
and of plausibility vis-à-vis the known facts of the Schreber
case. However, a difficulty that presents itself in the investigation is the question of how one may validly generalise from
the findings of the Schreber case to other cases of paranoia.
The correlation between the experiences of childhood and those
of adult life is not easy to parallel, and certainly not in detail.
Dr Schreber's medical writings may have led some at least of
his readers to use his methods of child-rearing, but we do not
have information available as to whether this led to other
instances of paranoia. More importantly, we cannot invariably
or even often find evidence of early 'persecution' in the case
histories of paranoid persons generally. However, if the link
with past reality were true only of the Schreber case, or of
only a few other cases, it would be necessary to return to the
traditional view of paranoia as, in general, altogether illusory.
The reality factor in a few cases would be of merely peripheral
interest, and not of general value. However, it is not in fact
necessary to draw this conclusion. The details of the Schreber
case may not be readily paralleled, but the question of difficulties in the father-child relationship - stemming perhaps
from a variety of causes - has a far greater potential for
generalisation. If difficulties in early relationship are in fact
central to this phenomenon, then we must look at other kinds
of early difficulties in relationship, to assess their potential
for leading to similar effects. What, in childhood, can block
love and cause hate? This must form the next step of our
investigation.

One of the potentially most pathogenic events of childhood is
the separation of the child from its parents at an early age.
There is an extensive literature on this; and, since this tends
to focus more attention on the mother than the father, we will
begin by considering separation-trauma in these terms, and
only later consider the possible significance of the difference
of gender of whichever parent is involved.

The tie between mother and child has ordinarily been established by the middle of the first year. If for some reason
separation occurs thereafter, this will evoke separation anxiety
and grief and set in train processes of mourning. Following the
studies of Bowlby (1952, 1956, 1960, 1961, 1963, 1973) and

other workers, it is evident that in the early years of life there
is a notable risk that the processes of mourning set in trâin by
such separation may involve unfavourable consequences for
later personality development, possibly resulting in more or less
permanent impairment of the ability to make relationships.

It is by now widely recognised that loss of the mother figure
in the period between about six months and three or four or
more years is an event of high pathogenic potential. The
reason for this, I postulate, is that the processes of mourning
to which it habitually gives rise all too readily at this age
take a course unfavourable to future personality development.
(Bowlby, 1960)

In considering responses to early loss and the nature of the
processes evoked by the loss of a love-object, certain phenomena
become apparent. Three main phases may be observed: initial
protest, which gives way to subsequent *despair,* and finally
leads to *detachment.* If the separation is temporary and reunion
takes place, these processes are not necessarily reversed
immediately. After brief separations, detachment usually gives
way after a few hours or days, and is commonly succeeded by a
period of ambivalent behaviour, when the child is alternately
demanding and hostile or rejecting towards his parents. However,
if the separation is longer or is repeated, it is possible that the
detachment may persist indefinitely (Bowlby, 1973), though it
is assumed that such rejection of the mother as a love-object
is not common (Bowlby, 1952, 1956). It is important to note that
detachment is considered (Bowlby et al., 1956) to be based on
the repression of the child's need for his mother. The attachment need does not merely disappear, but remains as a dynamic
force in the subconscious. The basis for this observation is
the excessive attachment behaviour that may suddenly appear
after a period of apparent detachment. The repression of the
need means that the need still persists and still requires to be
met.
The child may also show hostility at reunion. The child's anger
with the mother for staying away may lead to rejection of her,
i.e. rejection of the person for whom the child has an attachment need. Thus, rejection of the mother of itself implies the
repression of the attachment need. Bowlby et al. (1956) comment:

In general, the children who continue to repress their need
for attachment manifest the most marked hostility, whilst those
few who have an apparent absence of hostility come from the
group with excessive need for attachment.

Hostility per se would not be abnormal. Anger is a functionally
healthy response to the experience of trauma; and, with Fairbairn (1952), we may see hostility towards an attachment figure
as specifically a response to frustration. In the case of separation,

the purpose of anger is to promote reunion and to discourage
further separation. However, an excess of anger may militate
against its own purposes, as by maintaining the repression of
the attachment-need when the attachment-figure has become
available again.[8]

> Clinical experience suggests that the situations of separation
> and loss with which this work is concerned are especially
> liable to result in anger with an attachment figure that crosses
> the threshold of intensity and becomes dysfunctional. (Bowlby,
> 1973)

If anger of such intensity motivates the repression of the
attachment need, we may suggest that the danger to the growing
child's personality is likely to be considerable. The mourning-
reaction set in train by separation may of course be resolved
sooner or later, and in many cases it would seem that this
resolution has taken place: ambivalence may be worked through,
leading to the restoration of a good relationship. But what if the
mourning-reaction is not worked through? Bowlby (1963) mentions two variants of pathological mourning: repressed yearning
for the loved object, and repressed reproaches against it, i.e.
the repression of the two normal responses to separation and
loss. He considers each of these abnormal responses as of regular
occurrence in childhood. Moreover, should the loss be prolonged or permanent, he states that there is a greater danger
of one or more variants persisting, to the detriment of the
person's capacity for object relations. He does not, however,
detail specific disturbances stemming from such trauma apart
from an increased tendency to pathological mourning in the
adult (confirmed by the frequency with which adults prone to
pathological mourning have experienced loss of a parent in
childhood). However, our concern here is not to correlate
childhood mourning with adult mourning, at any rate with what
is overtly recognised as mourning in the adult. I wish to
suggest the possibility of linking childhood mourning with other
abnormal or pathological processes in the adult, which have
not hitherto been linked with unresolved and repressed infantile
trauma or recognised as derivatives of the mourning process.
Suppose that both repressed yearning for the love object and
repressed reproaches against it persist (a) together; (b) into
adulthood. Supposing such a state to become reactivated, what
form is it likely to take? An intense need for love, together with
an intense anger against the love-object, are indeed to be
found in some adults. Clinically, is this not the very condition
we were discussing earlier, viz. paranoia? I wish to hypothesise
that paranoia is the reactivation, in adult life, of unresolved
infantile trauma, caused by separation or other trauma that
similarly affected the child's libidinal capacity. Paranoia is very
precisely to be correlated with the twofold condition of pathological mourning in childhood that Bowlby refers to: both the

longing for the 'lost' object, and reproaches against it, have persisted unresolved. It not only involves but is, itself, the repressed reproaches of the young child against the source of love that 'betrayed' it, together with the repressed need for attachment which has persisted as a need still requiring to be fulfilled. Paranoia is the end-result of a pathological sequence, but it has not hitherto been recognised what the beginning of this sequence was.

If our hypothesis here is correct, this would reinforce our previous conclusion, based on the Schreber case, that paranoia is essentially a transference situation, not a mere projection; and that there is a reality factor involved which is of central importance. The paranoid does not actually project his own anger, but is accurate in ascribing hurtful behaviour to a love-source in early years. The paranoid's own anger is a response to this, and an entirely logical response when the facts are known.

It may be asked on what grounds separation trauma (as here discussed) and ill-treatment (as in the Schreber case) may both alike be considered causative of the paranoid phenomenon. The common aetiological factor is their ability to block the attachment to the needed love-source and to cause hate, as a twofold response to what is justifiably interpreted as a hateful action by the love-source. An important consideration to note is that such action by the parent need not have been wilfully harmful – separation may often be involuntary – but the point is that the child did in fact have justification for regarding the love-source as harmful, even if in a number of cases the traumatic situation did not actually involve any malicious intent.

From the foregoing analysis it becomes clear that the repression of the love-need is integrally linked with the repression of hostility towards the love-source. These are, in effect, the two sides of the same phenomenon. Neither can persist without pre-supposing the persistence of the other. Hostility towards the love-source blocks the ability to receive love from that source, thus resulting in an unmet love-need. The capacity for attachment to a love-source is damaged through trauma and through hatred for the agent of the trauma, viz. the former love-source. Since the unmet love-need implies a defensive detachment from the love-source, the persistence of the inability to receive love from that source presupposes the persistence of the defensive process.

When a young child is in the phase of detachment in the mourning process, strong defensive processes are at work (Bowlby, 1963). In psychoanalytic terms, there is counter-cathexis, rather than withdrawal of cathexis. A defensive barrier is erected. The nature of this barrier has not yet been sufficiently appreciated. Loss can evoke defence – and the defence is one against receiving love from the source of love that betrayed one. The most fundamental defence is an unwillingness to receive love. And, once this particular defence has

occurred as a response to trauma, it may persist as an incapacity
to receive love. On this hypothesis, if the trauma is sufficiently
severe, then, even if love is offered by the love-source subsequent to trauma, such love can no longer be received. The
sheer capacity to receive love, through attachment to a love-
source, has been repressed. And this repressed need for love,
which is normally met in the earlier years of life, persists unmet
into adulthood, as a need still requiring to be met. The paranoid's desire to receive love from the 'persecutory' love-source
is but the reactivation of this early infantile need, which has not
as yet been met, due to traumatic repression. The paranoid's
love-need is essentially the young child's need for love from its
parent. The repression in early childhood of the love-need and
of the hatred for the 'persecutory' love-source means that at
the conscious level there will be an apparent adjustment. The
child may seem to have 'got over' whatever the original trauma
may have been. But this superficial adjustment proves to be
based on massive repression; and to the extent that the
repression is lifted, the phenomena known as paranoid symptoms
will appear, as the tragedy of early years is re-enacted.

Of course, not all early trauma results in such consequences.
Trauma may be genuinely resolved, whether entirely or in some
greater or lesser degree. It is vital to give due weight to this.
However, at the same time it is important to bear in mind what
the consequences of unresolved trauma may be. If paranoia –
a condition which is generally regarded as mysterious, tragic
and almost incurable – is correctly identified as a reactivation
of a repressed, pathological mourning-reaction of childhood,
then the seriousness of the potential risk involved in childhood
trauma must never be underestimated.

2 THE STRUCTURES OF AMBIVALENCE

The paranoid position in effect involves an intense approach-avoidance conflict: an overwhelming unmet need for love is blocked by a defensive barrier of distrust and even hatred for the source of love that once 'betrayed' one. It is particularly to be noted that the sex of the 'persecutor' does not have to be the same as that of the paranoid. The original source of trauma may have been the parent of the same sex; but, equally, the traumatic event may have involved a parental love-source of the opposite sex. Freud's original theoretical position, which assumed that the 'persecutor' must be of the same sex as the paranoid, has to be revised in this respect. The paranoid position always involves a defensive barrier against a distrusted love-source, but that love-source may be of either gender. Either father or mother may, wittingly or unwittingly, have been the source of trauma to either a young son or a young daughter.

Thus far we have discussed the implications of the paranoid phenomenon without in fact explicitly discussing a central feature of Freud's hypothesis, viz. the link between paranoia and homosexuality. We have pointed out that the persecutory love-source need not be of the same sex as the paranoid, though in many cases the two do happen to be of the same sex. Whatever the sex of the 'persecutor' the basic structure of the paranoid phenomenon is the same: there is a need for love from a love-source that is seen as persecutory. However, when the persecutory love-source is of the same sex as the paranoid, this phenomenon is labelled homosexual. I have not previously used this particular term in the discussion, because I did not wish to prejudge the available data or to introduce premature evaluations. Our discussion of paranoia has so far considered the repression of the young child's normal need for love, consequent on trauma, and his hatred of the love-source that was the agent of such trauma. The repressed love-need of the young child may be reactivated in later years. This is the phenomenon which, when it happens to involve a love-source of the same sex, is labelled homosexual. On our data, this condition is essentially the reactivation of a thwarted infantile love-need, that has persisted unmet and hence still requires to be met. We are not, however, suggesting on account of this that homosexuality is not truly involved in this condition. What we are suggesting is that this is the so-called homosexual condition in its essence, viz. an unmet need for love from the parent of the same sex.

We may suggest that the present discussion offers us the possibility of drawing up a definitive critique of Freud's hypothesis. Studies subsequent to Freud confirmed that at any rate there is some coincidence of the conditions of paranoia and homosexuality, but it also became evident that in many instances this link cannot be established. Many paranoiacs do not give evidence of homosexual concerns, whether manifest or latent (Klein and Horwitz, 1949; Planansky and Johnston, 1962); and, on the other hand, many do show evidence of heterosexual concern. This evidence faced one with the question as to what extent there might be a link between the two conditions, of paranoia and homosexuality. What would be the nature of such a link - mere coincidence or some form of causal connection - and what would be the limits of its applicability? Studies of the incidence of these conditions have been of value, but ultimately can do no more than indicate that the two do not always coincide, and hence that Freud's hypothesis cannot be of universal applicability. However, despite this restriction of its applicability, the hypothesis as such was not disproved. What remained to be further investigated was the actual nature of the link between the two conditions. At the same time, this necessitates a greater understanding of the intrinsic nature of both paranoia and homosexuality.

The genesis of paranoia is seen to involve the formation, in a young child, of a defensive barrier against a love-source that is behaving hurtfully. In other words, the child represses his normal love-need, and the defensive barrier of mistrust and even hatred towards the hurtful love-source blocks the normal process of attachment to that love-source. If the love-source happens to be of the same sex as the child, whether a boy or a girl, the resultant condition may be denoted 'homosexual-paranoid'. If the love-source happens to be of the opposite sex from the child, whether a boy or a girl, the resultant condition may be denoted 'heterosexual-paranoid'. The one essential and constant factor of the paranoid condition is that it involves a repressed love-need. The gender of the mistrusted love-source is accidental.

However, in each of these two types of paranoia it should be noted that the repressed love-need is - as just explained - an intrinsic part of the structure of the paranoid phenomenon. Paranoia of the heterosexual type is, itself, a defensive barrier against a love-source of the opposite sex, i.e. the young child's need for love from the parent of the opposite sex has persisted repressed and hence unmet. Likewise with homosexual paranoia: this is, itself, the defensive repression of the young child's need for love from the parent of the same sex. In this way it may certainly be asserted that when homosexuality and paranoia do coincide, they are intrinsically linked, since they are but the two sides of the same phenomenon. To this extent we may agree with Freud. But we must differ sharply from the traditional hypothesis by insisting that not all paranoia is homosexual, i.e. that not all such distrust of a love-source is directed towards a love-source of the same sex. Not all paranoia is homosexual; nor - very importantly - is all homosexuality paranoid, i.e. not all unmet needs for love from the parent of the same sex are reinforced by a defensive barrier of the same magnitude and severity as that involved in the condition known as paranoid. There are other degrees of homosexuality, that may not be denoted paranoid. But more of this later.

The love-need that is repressed by a defensive barrier in the paranoid condition is in each instance to be correlated with a particular love-source, whether of the same sex or the opposite sex. Conversely, hatred for a particular love-source is to be linked back to a repressed love-need for that same particular love-source. To be more explicit, this implies that paranoia is misunderstood if it is seen solely in terms of negative emotions, viz. distrust and hate. These negative emotions are present, but their function has been the defensive repression of a love-need, in response to early trauma. The very existence of the defensive barrier implies the persistence of a need for love that has not yet been met (not met precisely because of this defensive barrier). The negative emotions of paranoia are but one side of this more complex psychodynamic structure. Strictly speaking, therefore, it is not appropriate to speak of the coincidence of paranoia with a pathological love-need, as if they were two separate conditions. As we have seen, they are but the two aspects of one and the same phenomenon. The love-need that is to be found in the paranoid is an integral aspect of the paranoid condition.

Conversely, a similar conclusion should be drawn with regard to the persisting love-need. The repression of the capacity for attachment has not only prevented the fulfilment of the child's love-need in the normal course of growth. So long as the defensive barrier is a dynamic force within the personality, i.e. in adult life as well as in childhood, it has the potential for hindering the fulfilment of the love-need. The very lack of fulfilment is, as we have seen, based on a defensive incapacity to receive love from the mistrusted love-source, i.e. the presence of such an unmet love-need implies the presence of an underlying conflict. In other words, the love-need of itself implies an ambivalence towards the needed love-source. The love-need cannot be isolated from the defensive process that has shaped it and caused it to persist unmet. Whether involving homosexuality or pathological heterosexuality (i.e. the child's unmet love-needs vis-à-vis the parent of the same or the opposite sex), the love-need is but one side of this larger phenomenon, in which the need for love and hate for the once-persecutory love-source are inextricably combined. The homosexual or heterosexual who 'becomes paranoid' is merely manifesting the dynamic processes underlying his particular love-need. The two emotions are not separable, but twin aspects of the same condition.

In practice, the term 'paranoia' has focused on the negative side of this larger and more complex phenomenon. The terms

'homosexuality' or 'pathological heterosexuality' would likewise
tend to focus on the love-need in abstraction from the underlying defensive barrier. Such definitions are misleading because
one-sided. For too long they have permitted people to assume
that two separate conditions are under discussion. They have
obscured the dynamics of the love-hate phenomenon in its
entirety; and, moreover, they have at the same time led to gross
inaccuracy in the definition of each side of this larger phenomenon. A particular example of this is to be found in cases where
the love-need is vis-à-vis a love-source of the same sex. Homosexuality has frequently been defined as 'love for the same sex'.
On our present analysis, it would be far truer to define it as
ambivalence towards the same sex. There is certainly a love-
need involved, but it is based on a defensive detachment from
the needed love-source. Similarly when the love-need is directed
towards a love-source of the opposite sex. In one and the
same condition we find both defensive detachment from a love-
source and an abiding need for attachment to that love-source,
which the defensive barrier has blocked. And, because defensive
detachment and the fulfilment of an attachment-need are mutually
incompatible in operation, the underlying conflict is considerable.

The defensive barrier against the fulfilment of a love-need is
involved in the very genesis of paranoia, and indeed is the
cause of the subsequent pathology. Paranoia as a clinical
phenomenon may become apparent only later in life, typically
after the age of 35. But it is vitally important to note that the
defensive barrier that is termed paranoid has been present from
early infancy, and has persisted from that time onwards. The
defensive manoeuvre may manifest itself only in adult life, but
it is most certainly not an adult manoeuvre per se. Rather, it is
the re-emergence of the young child's defensive response which
has subsequently been repressed.

Both the attachment-need and the hatred for the persecutory
love-source were repressed in early childhood. If the repression
fails in later years, either both aspects of this ambivalence may
become manifest or - as often - one side only of what is
essentially a unitary ambivalent structure. It is this latter
possibility that has contributed to the failure to realise that the
unmet love-need and the defensive barrier are essentially linked
and not separable phenomena. When Freud spoke of paranoia as
a defence against latent homosexuality, he was in effect indicat-
ing that often only the negative side of the ambivalence emerges
from repression. And the lifting of the repression implies not
the disappearance of the defence, but merely its overt manifestation, in full force.

Conversely, the defensive barrier might remain latent, while
the repressed need for love might come to the surface and
express itself in some form of attachment, in an attempt to meet
and fulfil the hitherto unmet need. However, since the defensive
barrier is still present in the psyche, there is always a risk that
it too may come to the surface, and lead to a growing negativity

towards the new love-source, as the full scope of the transference becomes manifest. Paranoid symptoms may either emerge
in isolation or else develop within the context of a restored
attachment, i.e. the negative side of the ambivalence may emerge
from repression by itself, or else as a consequence of the positive
side of the ambivalence having already emerged from repression.
Thus, too, both sides of the ambivalence may become manifest
at the same time.[1] Although in such instances the likelihood of
conflict is considerable, such a phenomenon does not contradict
our theoretical position, but merely manifests it in its fullest
dimensions. The simple Freudian position, which refers only to
latent homosexuality, is inadequate. The thwarted need for love,
whether repressed or manifest, is an essential characteristic
of the paranoid structure.

It should also be added that in a number of persons both sides
of the ambivalence are repressed. This is true, firstly, as a
generally applicable statement. We should remind ourselves
that persons who manifest either side of the ambivalence in adult
life are merely giving conscious expression to the intrapsychic
wound that they have borne repressed within them ever since
early childhood. Moreover, it is quite possible that in some
instances this twofold repression never comes to the surface.
Although such a statement is, of its very nature, incapable of
practical demonstration, the probability of its occurrence is
undoubted. The very length of the period of repression in those
individuals who do eventually manifest some aspect of the
ambivalence is a notable pointer. And if in some instances the
repression is adequately maintained, there may never be sufficient
material to attract clinical attention. However, from the nature
of the underlying intrapsychic trauma, such a person's capacity
for interpersonal relationships would not be that of a more
normal person, i.e. someone who had not been thus traumatised.
And it is likely that they, just as persons who do later present
overt symptoms, could in some cases be rather withdrawn
individuals, and maybe unhappy ones too. The persistence of
early trauma is always a human tragedy, whether or not it
manifests itself in socially disturbing behaviour.

We have so far structured our discussion around the arguments
of Freud, but it will be evident that studies subsequent to Freud
may also be criticised on the basis of the present hypothesis.

The position of Knight (1940) reverses that of Freud by seeing
love as a defence against hate, instead of hate as a defence
against love:

The drive to love and to be loved by the object of the homosexual wish is supported mainly by the intense need to
neutralize and erotize a tremendous unconscious hate.

We would see this as an incorrect statement of the relation
between these two powerful emotions. The drive for love is not
a defensive manoeuvre against an underlying anal-sadistic hate,

but rather is the young child's normal need for love that has been blocked by the hate that is an accurate response to early trauma. Knight asks two questions: What is the basis of the strong homosexual wish? And: Why is the paranoiac compelled to deny this wish so utterly? The answer to the first is that the young child's need for attachment to the parent of the same sex has been thwarted and hence has persisted as a love-need that still requires fulfilment. The second question may be answered by recalling the meaning of the paranoid phenomenon as a defensive detachment from a needed but hurtful love-source. The denial of the love-need is intrinsic to the genesis of the paranoid position. To ask why the paranoiac denies this love-need is merely to ask why the paranoiac is paranoid. As such, the question becomes redundant when one has understood how paranoia arises in the first place. Any denial of the love-need in adult life is but the de-repression and re-activation of the early defensive manoeuvre against the hurtful love-source.

Bak (1946) regards paranoia as delusional masochism – this in spite of the fact that he fleetingly acknowledges that the paranoiac is not infrequently a person who has experienced persecution in his past. Unfortunately, no attempt is made to link paranoid mechanisms with early social reality, and we are presented with an account of merely intrapsychic conflict, in which projection and other defence mechanisms are prominent. Bak speaks of the ego defending itself against a masochistic threat coming from the id, and of the projection of sadism on to a love-object. There is no understanding of how this might be not a projection, but the reactivation of a transference, in which the sense of being persecuted was in its origin an accurate response to persecutory behaviour.

Waelder (1951) likewise sees paranoid mechanisms as a means of dealing with troublesome instinctual drives, rather than as the correlate of difficulties in an actual interpersonal situation. Denial is regarded as the central mechanism of defence, and it is applied in order to resolve a conflict involving homosexual drives. It is explicitly stated that the denial is not in such an instance directed towards external facts, and herein Waelder's argument differs most significantly from our present hypothesis. We would see the need for love from a member of the same sex as an attachment need, the young child's normal need for attachment to the parent of the same sex. In the case of the paranoid, this attachment need has been blocked by a defensive detachment consequent on trauma from the love-source. It is the denial of the normal love-need, as a response to trauma, that creates the conflict in the first place. Denial is not the solution to the problem of an unacceptable drive, but is the means by which a normal attachment need is rendered incapable of fulfilment.

Ehrenwald (1960) speaks of symbiotic persons being faced with two alternatives: compliance with an omnipotent parent leading to passive homosexuality, or resistance and rebellion

leading to paranoia. We would not see these phenomena as
genuinely alternative to each other, but as intrinsically linked –
the two sides of the same phenomenon of ambivalence, arising
out of a defensive detachment from a needed love-source.
Genuine compliance could not result in a subsequent homosexual
response, since the capacity for such a response is created by
the thwarting of the attachment-need in the course of growth.
Compliance understood as unwilling submission could create a
defensive detachment, but as such it is not an alternative to
resistance, but would itself be the resistance to normal attachment that constitutes the paranoid phenomenon.

Schwartz (1963) suggests that the paranoid lacks the capacity
for self-referred responsibility. We should wish to disagree with
this verdict. It is not that the paranoid is unable to ascribe
blame or responsibility to himself. It is simply that in the
genesis of the paranoid position, the paranoiac does in fact
have justification for seeing the needed love-source as persecutory
In other words, the paranoiac's referral of responsibility to
someone else is an accurate appraisal of an early interpersonal
situation, and not a sign of incapacity.

The theories just detailed all assume the possibility of explain-
ing paranoia as a merely intrapsychic phenomenon. An attempt
at correlation with social reality was undertaken by Cameron
(1943a, 1943b, 1959a), but unfortunately this correlation focuses
on present reality rather than the early history of the paranoiac.
For this reason it must be regarded as unsatisfactory, in that it
is unable to do justice either to the meaning of the contemporary
distortion of reality or to the past trauma from which this subsequent distortion derives. Cameron sees delusion as a disorder
of interpretation arising from defective socialisation. Through
such misinterpretation, the paranoiac organises the world around
him into a pseudo-community. Imaginary functions are predicated
of real persons, based on fragments of their actual behaviour.
The paranoiac's own asocial behaviour contributes to the very
situation to which he then responds negatively.

Cameron's attempt at an explanation in terms of social reality
is recast in a more conservative form in his later writing on the
subject (1959a). The importance of the defences of denial and
projection is emphasised. The paranoiac sees people as hostile
due to the projecting of his own hostility on to them, which
results in a distortion of external reality. Indeed, the paranoiac
needs to experience hostility from outside as a defence against
being overwhelmed by his own, internal, aggression. Without
withdrawing his concept of the paranoid pseudo-community,
Cameron has in effect returned to a more traditional position by
allowing for the importance of intrapsychic conflict. And with
this one is faced yet again with the question of how such conflict
arises in the first place. The attempt at correlation with social
reality cannot be viably maintained unless linked with the
situation in which the paranoid position originated, not that in
which it may currently manifest itself. The quest for correlation

is a proper one, but must be undertaken with reference to the correct set of data.

All of these theories of paranoia may be considered inadequate through not doing justice to historical reality. Waelder makes mention of Freud's theory of an element of historical truth in psychosis, but even so he does not attempt to correlate paranoid symptoms with external social reality. Cameron's correlation with social reality ignores the need to consider past history. Other theories altogether ignore the need for correlation with social reality and present paranoia as a merely intrapsychic phenomenon. Hence it is not recognised that what we are dealing with is essentially a transference, rather than a matter of projection. Moreover, by isolating paranoid symptoms from the social context which gave rise to them, it is impossible either to explain them accurately or to do justice to the essential unity of the phenomenon of ambivalence. The thwarted love-need, and the defensive barrier against the love-source, are not separable phenomena, or alternatives to each other, but are integrally linked.

We must also differ from Klein et al. (1952), who regard the first three or four months of life of any infant as a 'paranoid-schizoid position'. What we are speaking of here is not a regression to an early but normal phase of development, but the abnormal blocking of normal growth, and at a somewhat later stage in the young child's development. Since we would see the genesis of the paranoid position in a pathological 'mourning' reaction in early childhood, we would follow the chronology of Bowlby and assign the period of vulnerability to after the establishment of a libidinal tie at about six months. The first few years of early infancy are the period in which there is a risk of trauma resulting in the establishment of a 'paranoid' ambivalence towards the needed but hurtful source of love.

We have discussed the basic structure of the paranoid phenomenon and its aetiology. Another matter of importance is to consider some of the derivatives of the basic phenomenon, and to link them to the given structure. How, on our present hypothesis, does one account for the symptoms characteristic of the paranoid syndrome?

Ideas of persecution are seen to be not the projection of the paranoiac's own unacceptable feelings of aggression, but the reproduction of an accurate perception of early interpersonal reality. Short of a full-scale systematised sense of persecution, there are also various types of behaviour that may be referred to this central, and essentially accurate, sense of 'having been wronged'. Prior to 'overt psychosis', i.e. the restoration to consciousness of the negative side of the repressed ambivalence, the latent paranoiac may in any case be a suspicious and mistrustful person. Such attitudes are comprehensible when seen as motivated by the early, unresolved trauma. Fundamentally, the paranoiac is suspicious of the love-source that did actually

'betray' or 'persecute' him (whether wilfully or involuntarily).
Likewise, the tendency of the paranoiac to be querulous and
even litigious is motivated by the wish to 'get back at' the love-
source that was genuinely hurtful and genuinely provided cause
for complaint, i.e. for 'litigation'. Hostility, too, is a logical
response to the hurtfulness of the love-source.

When, after a more or less prolonged period of repression and
consequent latency, the ambivalence begins to approach consciousness, the initial prodromal symptoms may be the development of ideas of reference. The sense of 'something is wrong;
something is the matter – *with reference to me*' is undoubtedly
true to intrapsychic reality as it has been shaped by early
trauma. Then, it would seem, this leads the paranoiac to find
out what it is that is wrong. The sense of something being amiss
has to be given some sort of concrete shape, and hence the
paranoiac is driven to look for this meaning in the events around
him. Thus, something that was true vis-à-vis early social reality
is reactivated in a contemporary context to which it does not
properly belong. Ideas of reference may develop into full-scale
referential systems as the drive to find the meaning of this
sense of unease persists and increases. We would regard it as
misleading to speak of these as delusional systems, since what is
involved is not in its essence delusional, even though the
accurate response to early social reality must be seen as
anachronistic when ascribed, incorrectly, to contemporary social
reality. It is hardly surprising that a so-called 'delusional'
system tends to be unshakeable, since the essential truth of the
underlying feelings would make it surprising if it were not held
on to tenaciously. The paranoiac may not do justice to present
reality, but we commit an equally serious mistake if we assume
that there is no possible correlation with reality at any point.
To persuade the paranoiac that his convictions are essentially
untrue, as distinct from misplaced, is not a proper therapeutic
goal, and one that deserves to fail in the attempt.

The essentially accurate idea of 'something is the matter with
me' takes on a special form when it is ascribed to bodily health.
The hypochondria that is a characteristic manifestation of paranoia
may be seen as stemming from this same underlying conviction.
The meaning of the intrapsychic wound is sought and found in
the person's state of health.

As the intrapsychic wound involves the blocking of the
capacity to receive love from a needed love-source, it should be
possible to explain megalomania and 'delusions' of grandeur as
a development from this. Receiving love in interpersonal relationships is the normal means of receiving a sense of personal worth.
Hence, if the former is blocked, the latter should be correspondingly affected. This is in fact what we find. The basic
assertion of megalomania is the proposition: 'I must be of great
worth.' However, this assertion arises precisely from the blocking of its means for fulfilment. The assertion is one of unmet
need, not of accomplished fact. And it is because the need is so

overwhelming - since it is a basic need that has for so long been
left unfulfilled - that the assertion is correspondingly strong.
Megalomania is thus the correlate of a severe inferiority complex.
It asserts, not 'I am of worth', but 'I should be of worth, but
have not in fact been granted this sense of worth.' The attainment of a sense of personal worth cannot be achieved by the
person concerned acting by himself, but is something that is
mediated through his relationships with other people. Thus,
disruption of an infant's capacity for attachment to a love-source
is bound in turn to have pathological consequences for the sense
of self-worth.

This presentation again contrasts with the Freudian understanding of paranoid overvaluation of the ego. Freud sees this as yet
another form of denial of homosexual love, i.e. 'I love him' is
contradicted by 'I love nobody,' which further implies 'I love
only myself.' On the contrary, we would assert that the
megalomaniac does not love himself, in any true sense of the
word 'love'. The assertion of grandeur is the assertion 'I des-
perately need to be valued - by others'. And underlying this
position is the defensive detachment of the young child from the
hurtful love-source, a detachment which prevented the child
from receiving the sense of worth that is normally mediated
through receiving love. The proposition involved is not 'I do
not love him,' but 'I cannot receive love from him or her.' And
if, in some paranoiacs, there is no overt megalomania, the
underlying wound to normal self-esteem is there nevertheless.

Ideas of passivity and the sense that one's thoughts are being
read might, we suggest, be yet another aspect of the reproduction of the psychic world of the young child. The infant vis-à-
vis the adult is in a position of powerlessness and passivity.
From such a position, it would not be surprising if the adult
appeared omnipotent and omniscient. If the emotions bound up
with early trauma may be accurately preserved and reproduced
in adult life, as we have here hypothesised, this would also
suggest the possibility of the preservation and reproduction of
other aspects of the infantile psyche, dating from that self-
same period in which the trauma occurred.

The basic principle being put forward in this discussion is
that the paranoid phenomenon in its various aspects is derived
from, and may be correlated with, the effect of trauma in early
infancy. This socially realistic interpretation is one that aims
to do justice both to past reality and subsequent pathology. In
this, it contrasts with the mainstream of psychiatric theory,
which has focused on the reality of present pathology and has
minimised or ignored the factor of historical truth; and contrasts
also with more radical presentations, which show some understanding of the truth-factor, but interpret this as a denial of
pathology.

Freud's descriptions of paranoid states are mistaken in his
ascribing them to the results of intrapsychic transformations,
i.e. as defences against unacceptable instincts rather than as

responses to an unbearable interpersonal situation. Freud takes as his starting-point the proposition 'I (a man) love him (a man),' and goes on to consider the ways in which this – which he considers to be an unacceptable instinctual drive – is denied. But Freud's starting-point proves to be incorrect. The actual starting-point may be represented by the proposition: 'He or she (a love-source of the same or opposite sex) behaved hurtfully towards me.' The starting-point is in the actual interpersonal situation; and the love-source involved need not be of the same sex as the young child, though in a number of instances this happens to be the case. Moreover, the defensive denial is not applied to an abnormal drive, but to a normal attachment need – the young child's need for love from the parent of the same or the opposite sex. However, the blocking of the capacity for attachment implies, in turn, that the instinctual drive or love-need that is normally fulfilled through such an attachment does in fact persist unfulfilled. In this secondary sense, one may speak of the denial of an instinctual drive. However, it is important that its derivative nature is recognised: the persisting love-need of the paranoid cannot be explained as an isolated intrapsychic phenomenon, but is to be linked with and seen as a consequence of the damage to the attachment-capacity, in response to a traumatic interpersonal situation. The instinctual drive as such is not to be labelled abnormal; but the blocking of the channel for its fulfilment, and hence the blocking of its actual fulfilment, is certainly abnormal.

As a corollary to this, it may be suggested that the unfulfilled love-need ought to be fulfilled, if the intrapsychic damage in the paranoid is to be truly healed. It is not the overt symptoms of psychosis that constitute the essential problem of paranoia, for these are merely the point at which the underlying problem begins to show signs that are socially disturbing. The central problem – one which has been in existence since the traumatic events of early infancy – is the unmet love-need and the defensive detachment from the love-source that has caused this normal love-need to persist unmet. Hence the twofold therapeutic goal must involve both the undoing of traumatic detachment and, through meeting the unmet love-need, the restoration of missing growth.

3 DISIDENTIFICATION

The defence against receiving love forms the central dynamic –
and the central problem – of the paranoid phenomenon, and this
is true whether the love-source in question is of the same sex
or the opposite sex. However, when the defence happens to be
against a same-sex source of love, there is an additional com-
plication. Relating to a parent of the same sex is important for
the process of identification. Hence any disruption in this
relationship will in turn affect the identificatory process. The
blocking of the capacity to receive love implies the blocking of
the ability to identify with the love-source. Moreover, just as
the unmet love-need presupposes a defensive detachment from
the love-source, similarly there is involved not a mere absence
of the identificatory process, but a defensive reaction against
identification. The aversion to the love-source implies an aversion
to identifying with the love-source – or, in other words, a disidentification from the love-source.
  Disidentification is thus a consequence of the pathological
mourning reaction in infancy that we would see as the genesis
of paranoia. This may be contrasted with Freud's suggestion
(1917 [1915]) of identification as a response to loss. Freud speaks
of the identification of the ego with the lost object, and this
hypothesis is invoked to account for two phenomena. First,
identification is made to account for the transformation of an
object-loss into an ego-loss. This seems superfluous. If in fact
the ego of the infant is fundamentally dependent on the parent,
the loss of the bond with the parent is per se an ego-loss. The
love-need that is met through attachment is of fundamental
importance for the growth of the young child's personality;
and, conversely, the disruption of the attachment is in itself
deleterious for the personality. It is the experience of loss per
se that is fundamental to the aetiology of the depressive position.
  Second, Freud links identification to hate for the lost love-
object. When identification with the object has occurred, self-
punishment can take place as a means of expressing hostility
towards the love-object. Freud regards identification as a means
of facilitating the expression of hatred. By contrast, we would
speak of hatred as blocking the capacity for identification.
Moreover, when reproaches are turned on the lost love-object,
they are directed outwards, towards actual love-sources, and
not towards internalised objects.
  In stating this, we are not necessarily assuming that there is
no possibility of identification taking place in some instances as

a possible response to loss, e.g. as an attempt to recover the lost object, when there is no defensive barrier to block such an attempt. However, the two factors specifically mentioned by Freud do not seem to require the hypothesis of identification to account for their occurrence. Indeed, the invocation of this hypothesis obscures both the significance of sheer loss, and the form taken by hatred for the lost love-object, i.e. paranoia rather than depression. And Freud does not begin to consider that a possible response to loss may be the actual rejection of the capacity for identification.

The aversion to identifying with a love-source of the same sex implies, in other words, an aversion to identifying with the same sex. On our given analysis, homosexual paranoia always involves this disidentificatory defence within its psychodynamic structure. This may in some instances take on a more concrete form. We would suggest that radical disidentification from a same-sex love-source, consequent on early trauma, is the cause of the phenomenon known as transsexualism.

In essence, we would not see any qualitative difference between transsexualism and paranoid homosexuality. It is important to bear in mind that not all homosexuality is paranoid, i.e. ambivalence towards a love-source of the same sex need not be reinforced by a defensive barrier of the severity known as paranoid, and the resultant love-need still to be met will not be as extensive as in paranoid homosexuality. However, when a defensive detachment from a love-source of the same sex is of the severity and magnitude that we have been discussing here, radical disidentification is said to be involved. Hence psychodynamically there would seem to be little difference between this most radical form of homosexuality and transsexualism. There may be some difference of degree, but there is certainly none of kind. In both instances the normal process of receiving love from, and hence identifying with, a love-source of the same sex, has been blocked by trauma in infancy. The difference between the two conditions lies in the subjective awareness of the fact of disidentification. Only in certain instances do we find a specific awareness of not being psychologically a member of one's anatomic sex, which is a sufficiently strong sense of aversion as to lead to the demand for de-classification from one's anatomic sex.

When radical same-sex disidentification has taken place, it becomes logical for a person to experience a sense of gender dislocation, and to press for reassignment in accordance with this sense of self-awareness. It would be improper to regard this as imaginary or delusional. Rather, it marks an accurate and realistic representation of how it feels to be a person in whom the process of same-sex identification has been blocked from an early age. There cannot be a same-sex identity where there has been little or no same-sex identification during the process of growth. Indeed, it would be illogical to expect this. An identity is the product of a process of identification, and in the absence of the cause one may not reasonably expect to find the effect. Transsexualism is not a denial of physiology (which the transsexual only too sadly acknowledges), but an accurate statement of tragic psychological reality.

The question of body image may itself be directly linked with disidentification. The transsexual is well aware of his physiological identity, and it is this that is a source of unhappiness for him. It causes unhappiness precisely in that it marks a likeness to that which the transsexual has, in the depths of his psyche, repudiated a likeness to and has been unable to identify with. So long as the defensive detachment from the same sex and the consequent inability to identify with it, remain embedded in the psyche, there will arise a distaste and even a revulsion for whatever is contrary to this awareness of disidentification. The repressed and deeply embedded aversion for the same anatomic sex that is a consequence of the original disidentificatory trauma results in an inability to tolerate same-sex likeness in one's own person. The demand for gender reassignment surgery is the logical culmination of the disidentificatory impulse.

The important point to note is this: one's own self-image is dependent on and derivative from one's ability to have identified with others of the same anatomic sex. Conversely, disidentification directly affects the person's self-image. The statement of an anatomic male, 'I do not experience myself as male' derives from, 'I cannot be like him, a male.' And similarly for the self-identity of anatomic women. The statement, 'I do not experience myself as female' stems from, 'I cannot be like her, a female.'

Homosexuals in general do not press for gender reassignment. In many instances, there is not in any case a sufficient degree of underlying disidentification to justify such a demand. Paranoid homosexuality does involve radical disidentification, but the defensive detachment from the love-source may or may not take on the form of a specific demand for de-classification. Most typically, the transsexual has been aware of gender dislocation since infancy. (This suggests that the awareness of disidentification may in such instances come to the surface actually at the time of trauma, or shortly thereafter.) The paranoid homosexual in general may not have experienced this express sense of disidentification in his growing years or even in his adult life, but in a number of cases there may be some fleeting sense of cross-gender awareness, stemming from the otherwise latent disidentificatory mechanism.

In bringing together radical homosexuality (i.e. paranoid homosexuality, whether latent or overt) and transsexualism, we would wish to note certain points arising out of the comparison. Paranoid homosexuality is a general category, of which transsexualism is a special instance. Even when paranoid homosexuality does not lead to a demand for gender de-classification, it nevertheless presupposes an underlying disidentification from the same-sex love-source. Hence this extreme form of homosexuality, no less than transsexualism, is fundamentally a problem of gender identity, rather than of sexuality as such. Conversely, transsexualism does not essentially differ from homosexuality in its most radical forms. This is not to suggest that transsexualism is in fact a defensive rationalisation of homosexuality, as has sometimes been suggested. True to its underlying psychodynamic structure, transsexualism makes manifest the disidentification that has caused it. It is entirely proper to continue to regard it as a problem of gender identity. At the same time, though, it would be right to link this with the point just made, that homosexuality in its extreme form marks a similar problem of gender identity. In both instances, the gender identity problem involves homosexual impulses, but in neither case is there any defensive manoeuvre against homosexual impulses as such. The fundamental defence, in each case, is against the same-sex love-source, which has resulted in the normal need for love from the parent of the same sex remaining unmet.

The chief point of difference between the homosexual and the transsexual has been taken to be the desire for gender reassignment. However, this difference proves to be more apparent than real, when the underlying psychodynamics are taken into account. In practice, it has often proved difficult to distinguish between the female homosexual and the female-to-male transsexual (Stoller, 1972, 1975). We would now suggest that male homosexuality and male-to-female transsexualism are similarly close conditions, at any rate as regards psychodynamic structure, if not in appearance. We would also suggest that the same aetiology applies for transsexuals of both sexes, i.e. radical disidentification from the same-sex parental love-source. The young boy disidentifies from his father, the young girl disidentifies from her mother, as a result of a defensive detachment from a love-source that has been experienced as hurtful. This further implies that we are unable to accept a theory of non-conflictual aetiology for male transsexualism. In both genders transsexualism is of a traumatic origin, indeed of a severely traumatic origin.

The possibility of defence against trauma in the aetiology of female transsexualism has been recognised (Stoller, 1975), but has not received significant theoretical development. More attention has been given to male transsexualism. The most prominent hypothesis to date has interpreted male transsexualism as the result of a non-conflictual learning process (Stoller, 1975). Hence male transsexualism has been regarded as a completely different condition from female transsexualism in their respective aetiologies. On considering the facts of the case histories, however, the similarities seem more impressive than the differences. Amidst differences of detail, it frequently becomes possible to isolate a common factor from such data as is available, viz. early separation - whether physical or psychological - from the same-sex parent. Even Stoller, whose theory is non-conflictual, presents evidence of the absence of the father in the early years of the male transsexual. It would be wrong to assume that all such early absence results in the young boy disidentifying from his father - clearly it does not always, or even frequently, do so. But it would be equally mistaken to assume - as Stoller's theory does assume in effect - that such absence cannot in itself be traumatic for the young child. Early parental absence is a potentially traumatic event. Hence those who wish to assert that it has not resulted in a traumatic entail in given cases, must assume the burden of proof for their statement.

In detail, the young male transsexual may have experienced any of a variety of traumatic events in his childhood. Walinder (1967) mentions foster homes; early illness; the parents' divorce; illegitimacy; the father leaving home; and the hospitalisation of the father. Likewise with the young female transsexual: foster homes, or parental divorce (Walinder, 1967); or the hospitalisation or emotional unavailability of the mother (Stoller, 1972; Green, 1974). The common factor in all these instances is the potential for causing a defensive detachment from the needed love-source of the same sex.

In considering the aetiology of female transsexualism, Green (1974) lists four factors as important: giving the child a male-derivative name; a stable, warm father; an unpleasant or emotionally unavailable mother; and the reinforcement of rough-and-tumble play. The first factor is irrelevant on our present hypothesis. It is in any case not proven that male derivative names are common among female transsexuals, and whether the incidence differs significantly from that in the general population. More importantly, the assignment of a name takes place at the time of birth, and the significant separation trauma occurs later, during the years of early infancy. There is no basis on which the two events may be linked. The fourth factor likewise seems insignificant, though not totally unconnected. Rough-and-tumble play may, indeed, in these cases stem from gender dislocation, but its reinforcement or non-reinforcement by the parents is irrelevant to the actual causation of the transsexual condition.

The second and third factors are relevant to the aetiology of transsexualism: the unavailability of the mother crucially so; and the warmth of the father as a very secondary factor, relevant only in connection with the former factor, and not otherwise. The unavailability of the mother results, in these instances, in a defensive detachment and disidentification. This by itself is the sufficient cause of the transsexual condition. The warmth of the father is not essentially a separate condition, since detachment from the mother of itself implies that the only remaining bond of attachment is to the father. And the girl's entirely normal attachment to her father becomes abnormal when coupled with this defensive detachment from the mother.

Stoller (1975) speaks of the emotional absence of the mother of

the female transsexual, and the frequency of emotional illness,
especially depression, in the mother. He couples this with a
father who is psychologically absent in two ways, i.e. he does
not support his wife in her depression, and he does not
encourage his daughter's femininity. Linking these two facts,
Stoller suggests that transsexual girls become masculine because
they substitute for their fathers in trying to rescue their
mothers from depression. By contrast, we would suggest that it
is the emotional absence of the mother that directly results in
disidentification in the daughter, i.e. the daughter's position is
essentially one of anti-femininity rather than of masculinity. A
quasi-masculinity may be considered the extreme manifestation
of this anti-feminine, i.e. disidentificatory, impulse. We do not,
therefore, see any attempt to 'substitute for the father' in this
process. And, whether or not the father attempts to encourage
his daughter's femininity, this is irrelevant once disidentification
has taken place. The crucial factor is the defensive detachment
from the same sex. So long as this persists, nothing done by a
member of the opposite sex can confirm a same-sex identity,
since there is no longer any process of same-sex identification
to be confirmed.

Likewise, once disidentification has actually taken place, the
personality of the same-sex parent also becomes irrelevant. We
must again differ from Stoller (1975), who states: 'Among the
factors that may assist a little girl in becoming feminine and
heterosexual are a feminine and heterosexual mother.'[1] Such a
statement presupposes a continuing process of identification,
which is precisely the factor that cannot in fact be presupposed.
If the girl is no longer able to identify with her mother, her
mother's identity is irrelevant, in that it is not being used as a
model for identification. What assists a little girl in becoming
feminine and heterosexual is an uninterrupted attachment to the
mother. It is the continuing capacity for identification that is
crucial.

Male transsexualism is, we suggest, an exactly comparable
process, involving a defensive disidentification from the same-
sex parent consequent on early trauma. Rather than the non-
conflictual imprinting of femininity (Stoller, 1975), it involves
a defensive anti-masculinity: an aversive impulse from the same
sex that may express itself in the form of quasi-femininity.
Stoller speaks of an absent father who does not protect his
son from the feminising effects of a close symbiosis with the
mother. Rather, it is the father's absence that itself results in
disidentification. This in turn implies that the boy's only remaining attachment is to his mother, but it is not the closeness to
the mother that causes transsexualism. Conversely, separation
from the mother would not make masculinity possible for the
transsexual boy. A defensive detachment from the same sex
cannot be made up for by undermining the attachment to the
opposite sex in addition. The only means of restoring masculinity
would be by undoing the defensive detachment from the same

sex and making up for the missing identificatory growth.
Our interpretation of transsexualism as stemming from disidentification implies not only a theory of traumatic origin. Significantly, it also implies that transsexualism is not - despite appearances - a cross-gender disturbance, but essentially a same-sex disturbance. It is a defensive detachment from the same (anatomic) sex; and it is this aversion from the same sex that manifests itself in an apparent sense of belonging to the opposite sex. The cross-gender awareness is not an illusion, but merely a misinterpretation. Underlying it is a genuine absence of same-sex identity, based on an aversive detachment from the same sex dating from early childhood. Similarly, homosexuality should not be defined - except secondarily - as a difficulty in relating to the opposite sex. Essentially it marks a difficulty in relating to the same sex. Its psychodynamic structure is same-sex ambivalence, and love for the same sex marks only one side of this ambivalence. Gender identity and (homo)-sexuality are intrinsically linked, in that it is the defensive detachment from the same-sex love-source that blocks the fulfilment of identificatory love-needs. It is through a continuing and uninterrupted love-attachment to a parental figure of the same sex that the process of same-sex identification takes place.

An absence of a same-sex identificatory attachment since early childhood implies a state of radically incomplete growth in the adult personality. However, the potential for restoration is not absent. The very capacity for so-called 'homosexual' love marks the attempt to fulfil the hitherto unmet needs for same-sex love and identification. These needs as such are in no way abnormal, but their lack of fulfilment in the normal process of growth is, however, abnormal. The capacity for same-sex, i.e. 'homosexual', love marks an inherent reparative tendency, towards making up for normal growth that has been missing. However, just as the defensive detachment from the love-source originally diverted these needs from their fulfilment, so likewise there is always a possibility of the reparative attempt being thwarted by the persistence of the defensive barrier. The need for same-sex love may be checked by the re-emergence of the other side of the same-sex ambivalence.

We have already considered this ambivalence with regard to paranoid homosexuality in general. We shall now consider it specifically in connection with the special form of paranoid homosexuality that is known as transsexualism. In many transsexuals something of the positive side of the ambivalence emerges from repression, i.e. the capacity for a same-sex attachment in which same-sex love-needs may begin to be met again. Female transsexuals, who in any case may be difficult to distinguish from lesbians, often have relationships with members of the same anatomic sex even before gender reassignment, as well as after. Male transsexuals may have had 'homosexual' relationships or desires before reassignment, and many enter such relationships, or would wish to do so, after reassignment.

Absence of such desires or acts would not controvert the given hypothesis, since it is assumed that the capacity for same-sex attachment was repressed at the time of trauma and may emerge from repression later as well as sooner, if indeed it emerges at all. Nor does a limited amount of heterosexual activity by the pre-operative male transsexual controvert our hypothesis. The physical capacity for heterosexual behaviour may be purely superficial, without implying a truly heteropsychologic personality structure. Moreover, any sense of closeness in the male transsexual's relationship to his female partner may perhaps stem from his sense of cross-gender identity. The closeness may be genuine, but it is not to be interpreted as comparable to the closeness experienced by someone who has completed the normal process of masculine identification.

In a number of cases, it would seem that the negative side of the ambivalence remains repressed. However, there is evidence to suggest that this is not always the case. A particularly interesting piece of evidence is the fact that in some cases where psychotherapy has been undertaken, an overt psychosis has appeared in the course of therapy. A good example of this is mentioned by Don (1963): after two months of therapy and some initial improvement, a male transsexual developed florid hallucinations and ideas of persecution, and was certified and hospitalised as a paranoid schizophrenic. This would seem to suggest that the relationship vis-à-vis a same-sex therapist initially enabled the positive side of the ambivalence to emerge, and that in this instance it was very shortly followed by a re-emergence of the negative side of the ambivalence. In other words, the patient at first was able to form a restored attachment to a same-sex love-source (i.e. the reparative urge, towards making up for missing growth), and this was presumably of sufficient intensity to facilitate the emergence of the defensive detachment from the love-source which had, since childhood, blocked the fulfilment of the love-need.

Persons who are overtly psychotic or who are judged to be latently psychotic are normally screened out by gender identity clinics. However, the very fact that such clinics must expect to receive a percentage of psychotic candidates is itself suggestive, and deserves further consideration. It might be regarded as unsafe to allow surgery for a psychotic candidate, but this consideration is strictly irrelevant to the question of whether or not such a candidate is genuinely transsexual. To say that a psychotic cannot be truly transsexual because he is psychotic, begs the question. Moreover, it would be analogous to saying that a psychotic could not be truly homosexual because he is psychotic, though the existence of a link between these two conditions is indisputable. It is this very same link that we are postulating in the case of the transsexual. And, because the basic mechanism involved is same-sex disidentification and ambivalence, we should not be surprised at finding a variety of clinical manifestations, according to which aspect of the ambivalence has become prominent. However, in any given case a partial manifestation of the underlying structure should not allow us to forget the nature of the phenomenon in its entirety.

Gittleson and Levine (1966) present evidence from a review of the literature that it is common for schizophrenics to experience a sense of confusion in sexual identity, and that ideas of change of sex occur in a number of cases. To see this as merely delusional is inadequate. We have already indicated that cross-gender awareness is more truly interpreted as the absence of a same-sex identity, and that such an awareness is psychologically accurate if in fact the normal process of same-sex identification has not taken place. May this not apply in the cases here referred to? The awareness of this absence of identification may or may not be sufficiently strong as to lead to a demand for gender de-classification, but there is no a priori reason for assuming that the awareness as such is inaccurate or in itself pathological. What is pathological is the fact of missing growth, not the awareness of this fact, which is entirely appropriate to the given circumstances.

Krafft-Ebing (1899) speaks of paranoid men with delusions of persecution who believed they had become women. Fortineau et al. (1939) mention a similar case. Green (1969) speaks of an overtly paranoid schizophrenic who wanted gender reassignment.[2] Medication resulted in the control of his paranoid symptoms, but had no effect on his cross-gender orientation. Schreber himself, that most celebrated of paranoiacs, had doubts as to his sexual identity, with the impression of having a feminine body and being changed into a woman. This keen awareness of disidentification suggests that Schreber might be regarded as at least a borderline transsexual.

The literature on autocastration provides further material for reflection. Self-castration, that radical act of gender de-classification, is considered not uncommon among psychotics. Of particular interest are the cases mentioned by Blacker and Wong (1963). The first case is one of acute homosexual panic with many paranoid ideas. The three other cases all mention a strong sense of feminine identification, with or without a history of homosexual desires or practices, and in one case with paranoid tendencies being apparent. The discussion concludes by stating that these men differ from transsexuals, because of their schizophrenic tendencies and because their sense of cross-gender identity is insufficiently clear and persistent. Neither consideration is incompatible with our present understanding of trans-sexualism. The 'schizophrenic tendencies' evidently refer to the emergence of the negative side of the ambivalence; and the awareness of disidentification is not as marked as in more obvious cases of transsexualism. But the data presented clearly suggest an underlying disidentificatory structure, and hence there seems little to distinguish these cases from accepted instances of transsexualism.

Lukianowicz (1959a, 1962) discusses cross-gender behaviour in psychotic episodes. And Pauly (1969),[3] just as Lukianowicz, raises the question of whether cross-gender behaviour and identity form part of a long-standing process or are the acute manifestation of a schizophrenic reaction. We would see these two possibilities not as genuinely alternative phenomena, but as two forms in which the same phenomenon may be manifested. Disidentification of this severity always originates in early childhood. It may become apparent immediately, but need not do so until much later, if at all. Awareness of disidentification may emerge in isolation, or within the context of one or other aspect of the same-sex ambivalence involved in disidentification. If linked with the positive side of the ambivalence, disidentification appears in the context of a homosexual relationship. If linked with the negative side of the ambivalence, disidentification may emerge in what is termed a psychotic illness. But all these possibilities are manifestations of the same underlying phenomenon.

It is not that transsexualism is a manifestation of psychosis, but that an overt psychosis is a possible form of manifestation of the underlying state of disidentification. Indeed, from our discussion of paranoid ambivalence and its various manifestations, we might do well to redefine the concept of psychosis as one of radically incomplete growth, stemming from and maintained by the persistence of unresolved early trauma. This is not 'madness', in the sense of something illogical or inexplicable. Nor is it unrealistic, since the representation of psychological reality is seen to be all too tragically accurate.

At this point, however, we must go on to remind ourselves that not all same-sex disidentification is of this order of severity. The defensive barrier against a love-source of the same sex need not be as intense as in cases denoted paranoid. And the unmet love-need, i.e. the missing identificatory growth, need not therefore be as extensive as in cases of radical disidentification. There is a spectrum of homosexuality, i.e. there are many instances in which the degree of same-sex ambivalence is much less marked. We have already stated that not all paranoia is homosexual; we must now complete this delimitation by asserting its already obvious complement, that not all homosexuality is paranoid.

An interesting line of thought in the psychiatric literature recognises that many cases presented as homosexual in fact involve non-sexual questions, e.g. dependency and aggressiveness vis-à-vis the same sex. Thompson (1947) speaks of instances where homosexuality is but one of the manifestations of a character problem, and states that the homosexuality tends to disappear when the more general character disturbance is resolved. Thus, homosexuality may present itself in conjunction with a fear of adult responsibility, a fear of the opposite sex, a need to defy authority, a marked dependency on the same sex, or hatred for or competitiveness with the same sex. Thompson concludes that in such cases homosexuality is never the cause

of the overall neurotic structure, even if it may contribute some
secondary problems to it.

This line of thought is further developed by Ovesey (1954,
1955a). He takes up the point made by Thompson and others
that non-sexual problems are often covertly expressed in homosexual relationships. He, like they, wishes to restrict the term
'sexual' to behaviour with orgastic satisfaction as its aim. On
this basis, Ovesey concludes that homosexuality must refer to
sexually motivated behaviour alone. Dependency strivings and
power strivings, even if they use sexual behaviour to achieve
their goals, must be regarded as pseudo-homosexual. The great
majority of so-called homosexual anxieties are, he states, motivated by strivings for dependency and power; and it is mistaken
to interpret this pseudo-homosexual conflict as evidence of true
homosexuality, i.e. of sexually motivated behaviour, as just
defined.

While accepting the data of Ovesey and his predecessors, we
should wish to differ with the given interpretations and conclusions. We would agree that strivings for dependency and
power vis-à-vis the same sex are not essentially sexual. However, the conclusion we would draw from this is that homosexuality itself is not essentially a sexual phenomenon. We
would see the questions of power and dependency as central,
and their eroticisation as secondary and non-essential.

Authority problems vis-à-vis the same sex, whether involving
defiance or hatred or competitiveness, may all be considered
manifestations of a defensive detachment from the needed love-
source. Likewise, dependency problems vis-à-vis the same sex
mark the love-need that has remained unfulfilled due to the
defensive barrier against libidinal attachment. Thus, authority
problems and dependency problems are exactly complementary,
as the two sides of the overall phenomenon of same-sex ambivalence. Paranoid homosexuality is but the most radical form of
this ambivalence: its need for love is an extreme form of the
dependency problem, and the hatred for the needed love-source
is a very marked authority problem, with which the problem
of unfulfilled dependency needs has to be correlated. Non-
paranoid homosexuality is marked by lesser degrees of ambivalence towards the same sex, but the difference is fundamentally
one of degree rather than of kind. Homosexuality, of whatever
degree, is marked by a psychodynamic structure of same-sex
ambivalence.

It is the term 'homosexual' that is misleading, since it tends
to focus on only one side of this ambivalence. Homosexuality
includes love for the same sex, but this is not the full definition
of the given phenomenon, even if one side of the ambivalence is
often more apparent than the other. Thus, we would disagree
with Thompson's conclusion that homosexuality is never the
cause of the overall neurotic structure. Homosexuality - understood as same-sex ambivalence - is itself 'the overall neurotic
structure', whether or not erotic impulses happen to occur in

connection with this. Freud (1905) stated that 'neurosis is the negative of perversion.' We would re-apply this specifically to our understanding of homosexual ambivalence by stating that a defensive detachment - however manifested - is the negative of an unfulfilled love-need. And, when this ambivalence happens to be radical, it is to be correlated not with neurosis but with psychosis.

In contrast with Ovesey's conclusions, though not with his data, we have stated that homosexuality is not an essentially sexual phenomenon. In all cases it involves libidinal needs, but the eroticisation of such needs is not essential and may in fact never take place, though in a number of cases it is clear that this does happen. The non-sexual factors of authority and dependency problems prove to be essential to the statement of the libidinal problem. The unfulfilled love-need, i.e. the dependency factor, has only become problematic through the defensiveness towards the potential love-source which constitutes the authority problem. Moreover, since all homosexuality involves ambivalence towards a love-source of the same sex, this of itself implies that all homosexuality is a gender identity problem. Same-sex identity is normally built through a libidinal bond with the same sex, i.e. with the parent of the same sex. Conversely, the identificatory process is checked to the extent that the capacity for such a libidinal bond is affected. There are, of course, greater and lesser problems of gender identity. However, it would not be right to restrict the term to problems of radical de-classification alone. It is proper to speak of a problem of gender identity in any instance where the process of same-sex identification is in any degree incomplete.

To conclude our discussion of disidentification, we must consider its implications for the normal process of identificatory growth. The first love-object for girl and boy alike is the mother, but this is the same-sex parent for the girl and the opposite-sex parent for the boy. The heterosexual position implies by definition an attachment to the opposite sex - for the boy, a love-object of the same sex as his first love-object; for the girl, a love-object of the opposite sex to her first love-object. Hence the gap between the child's first attachment and the heterosexual position of mature years is bridged by stating that the girl has to change her love-object, indeed to abandon it, while the boy keeps his love-object unchanged (Freud, 1925; 1933 [1932]). However, from our earlier discussion this would seem to be a misleading and incorrect statement of the way in which this development takes place. For the girl it is precisely the abandonment of the first love-object that is pathological. This change of love-object is the essence of the radical disidentificatory trauma we have just considered. It is the retention of the first love-object, the mother, that is essential for the girl's normal identificatory growth. Freud (1933 [1932]) asks how the girl passes from an attachment to the mother to an attachment to the father, i.e. from a masculine phase to a feminine phase.

This question is self-contradictory. If the girl does make such an exchange of attachments, she has in fact passed from a feminine phase to an anti-feminine, quasi-masculine phase. The attainment of femininity requires the first love-object to be retained, since it is in this attachment that identificatory needs are met and thus a same-sex identity is attained.

Likewise if a boy retains, and does not change, his first love-object, this is pathological, in that it marks a blocking of the same-sex identificatory process. It is normal, and necessary, for the boy to exchange his first love-object for a love-object of the same sex. It is only this new attachment that permits the attainment of a same-sex identity, and conversely it is the blocking of this attachment that thwarts the process of identification. Disidentification in the boy implies a regression to the first love-object; in the girl it implies the loss of the first love-object. Thus, the boy's normal development implies a change of love-object, and the girl should retain her first love-object for normal growth. In contrast with the traditional psychoanalytic position we must state that it is the boy's process of growth that is more complex, and the girl's is the simpler path of development.

To behave heterosexually as an adult, one must have become *heteros* - truly *other* than the love-object one relates to. The similar gender of the boy's first object (mother) and of his final object (wife) must not mislead one into overlooking the complexities of the intermediate stage of development, since without this intermediate stage the final object-choice does not become possible. Exchange of the first object must precede the re-attainment of the female as truly other. It is not merely the boy's choice of object that must be considered, but his own identity vis-à-vis the object. The choice of love-object is determined by the fulfilment or non-fulfilment of one's own identity. When same-sex identificatory needs have been fulfilled, one has become a psychologically complete member of one's own sex and by this same fact a person who is able to relate as truly other to a member of the opposite sex. However, when the same-sex identificatory process is still incomplete, there remains a need to fulfil this process. Hence, the reparative urge dictates a reparative choice of love-object, i.e. the restoration and continuation of a libidinal bond in which same-sex identificatory love-needs may be fulfilled.

The capacity for heterosexuality is the normal end of the same-sex identificatory process. Indeed, it is not to be considered as something separate from this process, but is itself to be defined in these terms. Heterosexuality is the ability to relate to members of the opposite sex as a psychologically complete member of one's own sex. Heterosexuality implies that same-sex identificatory needs have been met, and consequently that relationships do not require to be governed by a reparative urge towards the fulfilment of one's own identity. The homosexual capacity involves the drive towards the fulfilment of same-sex identificatory needs, i.e. ultimately the homosexual capacity is itself the drive towards heterosexuality. It marks the inherent reparative urge based on the fact of incompletion and the consequent striving towards completion (of same-sex identity). Just as heterosexuality is the normal end of this process, so likewise the fulfilment of same-sex, i.e. 'homosexual', needs, is a normal and necessary part of this process. But it is not meant to be the end of the process: the homosexual drive is instrumental to the goal, rather than the goal itself. However, it is a necessary means to the given goal, and it cannot be bypassed. True heterosexuality is based on the fulfilment of 'homosexual' needs. Conversely, unless and until these 'homosexual' needs are fulfilled, there can be no truly heteropsychologic personality structure.

4   THE MALE HOMOSEXUAL

The psychodynamic structure of homosexuality is one of ambivalence – of greater or lesser degree – towards the same sex. Thus, in the male homosexual we should expect to find certain components of this ambivalence, as follows. A defensive detachment from the same-sex love-source will be marked by hostility, whether latent or overt, towards the father and towards other members of the same sex. Such other persons would particularly include authority figures, as obvious father-substitutes; and also homosexual partners, since in the context of a renewed libidinal attachment there is always the possibility of the other, negative side of the ambivalence becoming manifest, as the transference develops.

Moreover, such a defensive detachment implies a blocking of the normal identificatory process. In the more radical degrees of disidentification, this absence of masculinity – which is based on a defensive anti-masculinity – may be experienced as a sense of femininity. In the less radical degrees of disidentification, there is not likely to be any sense of cross-gender awareness, since there has been sufficient of the identificatory process to produce a viable sense of same-sex identity.

However, whether or not there is an actual sense of femininity, there should in any case be what is often termed a fixation on the mother. What is meant by this is that, when there is a defensive detachment from the father, the only remaining channel for attachment is to the mother. To be attached to the mother is in itself entirely normal. What is abnormal is that this should become the only channel of attachment. A mother-fixation in the male is not an abnormal attachment to the opposite sex, but an abnormal detachment from the same sex.

Detachment implies that the love-needs which are normally fulfilled in the context of an attachment remain unmet. At the same time, there is a reparative urge towards the restoration of the broken attachment, and hence towards the fulfilment of the unmet love-needs. The capacity for a homosexual love-response is itself the expression of this reparative drive. Its aim is not to meet abnormal needs, but to meet normal needs which have – abnormally – been left unmet in the given instances. The longing for masculine love is the longing to become fully masculine, since the identificatory process takes place through the medium of a libidinal bond. The desire to attain masculinity is thus another component of the homosexual phenomenon. We shall now consider each of these components in some detail.

The classic example of homosexual hostility to the father-figure, and indeed the most radical example, is that of paranoid homosexuality, as in the Schreber case. However, it is clear that aggression also has an important role to play in the object-choice of homosexuals in general (Nunberg, 1938). Fenichel (1945a) speaks of their unconscious hostility for and fear of the father, and says that in the context of a homosexual relationship such persons 'unconsciously may be governed by more or less hostility toward the father figures they are submitting to.'[1] Bieber et al. (1962) detail a variety of cases in which the male homosexual had a poor relationship with his father during his growing years. It is noteworthy that in cases where the father had been actually hostile, as distinct from indifferent or ambivalent, the homosexual partner was invariably identified with the father who had been hated and feared.[2] It is thus hardly surprising that such relationships should involve hostility and instability and impermanence. On the evidence presented, Bieber et al. conclude that much in the homosexual relationship is destructive.[3] In the terms of our own hypothesis, this implies that the defensive detachment from the needed love-source may at any time reassert itself to thwart the reparative urge. The problem is not merely one of restoring the needed attachment, but of maintaining it in spite of the persistence of the defensive reaction. It is not that homosexual love as such is destructive, but that the persisting sense of aversion to the love-source may at any time disrupt the restored attachment again.

In some instances, the negative side of the ambivalence may be so deeply repressed that it may not readily emerge into consciousness. This would seem to be more true of the paranoid end of the homosexual spectrum, where the negative side of the ambivalence may not emerge or not fully emerge until well on into adult years, if at all. It is the lesser degrees of negativity that tend to become more apparent, as in non-paranoid homosexuality. These may become manifest in the context of a libidinal bond, i.e. in such cases the negative side of the ambivalence is linked with the re-emergence of the positive side of the ambivalence. Or the negative side of the ambivalence may re-emerge in isolation, in which case it is likely to be expressed in the form of authority problems, i.e. the link with a libidinal need will not be overtly apparent here.

Such authority problems may become manifest in individuals or, sometimes, collectively. Homosexuals and heterosexuals are usually well mixed within society as a whole, whether or not they are aware of each other's sexual identity. Hence the possible effect of homosexual authority problems will be diluted (not to mention that in many homosexuals such problems will either not be conscious or not very marked or may be largely restricted to the context of libidinal relationships. Moreover, heterosexuals may have their own authority problems, though in such instances these are not - by definition - linked with their gender identity.) However, in societies that cater exclusively or largely for homosexuals, a different pattern may at times become apparent. It has struck a number of observers and participants that homosexual groups tend to have an unusually high incidence of instability and of authority problems. I should like to suggest that this phenomenon becomes explicable when it is realised that most of the persons involved have latent or overt authority problems in some degree, i.e. the defensive detachment we have already discussed. Under the circumstances, the high incidence of such problems within the group as a whole is hardly surprising. The potential for this is always present.

We should remind ourselves that this hostility to members of the same sex is realistic in its origin, whether stemming from early trauma or from subsequent difficulties in the parent-child relationship. The causative factor may be neglect or hurtful behaviour on the part of the parent; or it may be some action that was unintentionally traumatic, as is often - though not always - the case in early separation. In all these instances the child had reason to feel traumatised, whether or not the traumatic event was wilful. And, whatever the details of the particular trauma, the common factor in every case is the blocking of the needed libidinal attachment, in that the child's actual capacity for attachment is affected. It is not the mere absence of attachment, but a defensive detachment, that constitutes the central problem - though this in turn implies that the needs normally met through attachment remain unfulfilled. This defensive position, with its concomitant hostility, is subsequently manifested as a transference reaction, in that the residues of the past relationship are reactivated in the context of present reality. Paranoid homosexuality is but the extreme example of this. In all the lesser degrees of same-sex ambivalence, the reactivation of past interpersonal reality is likewise involved, and hence the designation of transference is appropriate. (Within a specifically therapeutic relationship one may look for a *controlled* transference. However, it is not the therapeutic context that is constitutive of the transference, but rather the inherent tendency of the human personality to reproduce the problems of the past - in a variety of contexts - for so long as they remain unresolved.)

Hostility to the father or to other persons of the same sex may have as its correlate a sense of injustice experienced in relation to these same persons. This again is essentially realistic in its origin. The love-source was hurtful, whether deliberately or unintentionally, and hence a sense of being wronged is readily comprehensible. Bergler (1961) speaks of 'injustice collecting' as one of the most salient character traits of the homosexual. He speaks of how this problem appears most particularly within the context of long-term homosexual relationships. When these are attempted, Bergler states that 'unsurmountable conflicts of the injustice-collecting type invariably appear.'[4] Interestingly, he links this with the mother-fixation of the male homosexual, and regards injustice-collecting as directed

'historically and genetically' towards the mother, not the father.[5]
As will become evident presently, we would regard this as a
misinterpretation of the mother-fixation. Such a fixation is
secondary to a defensive detachment from the father, and
injustice-collecting is essentially and realistically directed at
the same-sex figure from whom the homosexual has become
detached. Injustice-collecting in homosexual relationships is,
straightforwardly, the reactivation of this same-sex conflict.

Where the identificatory process has been radically blocked,
a sense of 'femininity' may be experienced. If the sense of cross-
gender awareness is strong and persistent, this would be the
transsexual condition, which we have already discussed in some
detail. Where such awareness of the absence of masculinity is
somewhat less marked, but still experienced to some extent as
'femininity', we may have what Ferenczi (1916) would designate
as the 'subject' homosexual (which may originally have included
transsexuals, prior to the isolation of this condition). Cases of
this type are mentioned by Henry (1950), Bieber et al. (1962),
and throughout the literature generally. Ferenczi's other
category, of the 'object' homosexual, would imply a lesser degree
of disidentification. The reparative urge stemming from incomplete identification is still apparent in the choice of a same-sex
love-object, but there is a sufficient sense of same-sex identity
established so as not to involve any cross-gender awareness.

The sense of femininity in the man does not, however, stem
from an identification with the mother, and to suggest this is to
misinterpret the essential nature of the homosexual phenomenon.
The primary dynamic is same-sex disidentification. This is not
to deny that a fixation on the mother, as the opposite-sex parent,
is involved; but it is to insist that this is secondary to and
consequential on a detachment from the same-sex parent. The
prominence of an effect should not be allowed to obscure the
true nature of the cause.

The concept of the mother-fixation of the male homosexual has
been a standard ingredient of psychoanalytic theory since Freud,
and it has been ascribed the kind of primary importance that we
would regard as misleading. Bychowski (1945) speaks of a homosexual identifying with the mother, and thus submitting to
father substitutes and making them love him. Likewise, Fenichel
(1945a) speaks of a homosexual man identifying with his mother
in respect of loving men. The basis of femininity in men is 'an
identification with the mother in regard to instinctual aim'.[6]
This confuses the issue. The male homosexual disidentifies from
his father, as a result of which the attachment to the mother
becomes paramount. However, the homosexual's love for men is
but the boy's thwarted love for his father, i.e. it is a masculine
and an identificatory love which is intimately linked with the
building of the boy's gender identity. Hence it is in no way
analogous to the love of the female for the male, since this latter
kind of love does not aim at fulfilling an incomplete gender
identity, but rather presupposes the completion of the identi-

ficatory process. The capacity for homosexual response is to be
directly correlated with same-sex disidentification, in that it
marks the reparative urge towards the restoration of the identificatory process. We must disagree with Fenichel's statement
that 'the probability of homosexual orientation is increased the
more a boy tends to identify with the mother.'[7] It is not identification with the parent of the opposite sex, but disidentification
from the parent of the same sex that is central.

A detailed study of the male homosexual's relationship with
his mother is presented by Bieber et al. (1962). Here it is
stated that 'an intimate mother-son dyad occurred frequently,
and . . . this intimate pairing was often associated with
restrictive and binding maternal behavior.'[8] Such behaviour is
characterised as dominating or seductive or overprotective or
discouraging of masculine activities. This intimacy of relationship permits the designation of the homosexual's mother as
close-binding-intimate ('the CBI mother'). At the same time,
evidence is offered that detachment and often hostility are the
most conspicuous traits of the fathers of homosexuals. Concretely,
this might involve the father spending little time with his son,
or not showing him affection, or showing preference for his
other children. Either directly hurtful behaviour, or neglectful
behaviour, or both, may be involved, but in every case the
result is an impaired relationship between father and son. That
this is significant in the aetiology of male homosexuality should
be evident from Bieber's statement that, out of a sample of 206
male homosexuals in psychoanalysis, only eight had fathers who
related warmly to them.[9] Characteristically, the father of the
homosexual would tend to be - in order of frequency - detached-
hostile, detached-indifferent, detached-ambivalent, or absent
altogether. Thus, in most instances the father would be present
in the family, but psychologically absent, at least as regards his
relationship to the son who was later designated homosexual.

Bieber does speak of the importance of identification with the
same sex, and states that a detached father has an adverse
effect on this identificatory process.[10] However, the maternal
relationship is ascribed central importance, and difficulties in
the father-son relationship are subordinated to this. It is said
that a warmly-relating father protects the son from engulfing
maternalism, while a detached father does not do so.[11] This again
suggests a confusion of cause and effect. If a poor father-son
relationship results in a defensive detachment from the father,
this of course leads to an undue prominence of the mother-son
relationship. However, this does not imply that the mother-son
relationship is pathological per se (though it may be as good or
as poor as mother-son relationships are generally). What is
pathological is the fact that such a relationship, which may be
largely normal per se, is in such cases isolated from a normal
father-son relationship. A warmly-relating father does not 'save'
his son from defects in the mother-son relationship, but
balances the one attachment by providing the relationship which

is its essential complement. But the source and focus of any pathology is the defensive detachment from the father, and it is this that requires to be remedied. The fact that - as Bieber states - a warmly-relating father in combination with any kind of mother precludes the development of homosexuality, is entirely congruent with our hypothesis that it is the father-son relationship that is of central importance. Bieber states:[12]

> The 'classical' homosexual triangular pattern is one where the mother is CBI and is dominant and minimizing toward a husband who is a detached father, particularly a hostile-detached one. From our statistical analysis, the chances appear to be high that any son exposed to this parental combination will become homosexual or develop severe homosexual problems.

We should wish to reshape this statement by asserting that the primary pattern for homosexual development is dyadic rather than triangular. Difficulties in the father-son relationship are central. Since these in turn affect the balance of the mother-son relationship, it becomes possible - secondarily - to speak of a triangular imbalance. But this triangular imbalance is an effect of dyadic difficulties, and hence may not be regarded as on a par with the latter. The triangular imbalance is not in itself causative of a homosexual development, even if - subsequent to dyadic disturbance - it is apparently the context in which such a development takes place. The central factor is not a CBI mother in combination with some kind of detached father. It is the detachment of the father that is central, and that is directly causative of the homosexual development. Imbalance in the attachment to the mother is an effect of the disturbed father-son relationship, but such a mother-son attachment is not causative of homosexuality. It may be regarded as either an effect of homosexuality, i.e. as an effect of a defensive detachment from the father, or as part of the effect that is homosexuality, i.e. of the position consequent on the defensive detachment from the father. But the dyadic disturbance of the father-son relationship is, and remains, primary.

We would agree with Bieber that homosexuality is not constitutional, but rather the outcome of pathologic parent-child relationships (though with the reminder that such difficulties need not always stem from wilful misbehaviour on the part of the parent). Our interpretation of what is and what is not pathological differs from Bieber, though the difference is not one of evidence but of the assessment of what conclusions ought to be drawn from the given evidence. We must disagree most particularly with Bieber's overall conclusion that his study provides convincing support for the understanding of homosexuality as a fear of heterosexuality.[13] On the contrary, it would seem to provide ample evidence for our hypothesis that homosexuality is essentially a disturbance in the capacity for relating to the same sex.

Bene (1965a) suggests that the mother-fixation of the male
homosexual may imply, not a stronger attachment to the mother,
but merely a poorer relationship with the father. The quality
of the mother-son relationship recalled by male homosexuals is
no more intense than that recalled by married men, and Bene
concludes that there is need to pay attention to the role of the
father. It is unfortunate that her suggestion, with which we
entirely agree, has not had much impact on the mainstream of
psychoanalytic thought. The predominant concept has been,
and still is, that of fixation on the mother, rather than of
detachment from the father.

Bychowski (1945) speaks of identifying with the mother out of
a wish not to lose her. In contrast with this, we must assert
that apparent identification with the mother stems from the actual
loss of the bond with the father. The question of losing or not
losing the mother does not arise. The so-called mother fixation
is but the converse of the disruption of the bond with the
father, and it is this loss that is central to the problem.

Bergler (1961) describes the homosexual relationship as a
defence mechanism, with the aim of escaping the mother-
attachment. The male homosexual is in flight from the mother
and this results, secondarily, in the ascription of sexual attrac-
tiveness to men. This would seem to state the problem the wrong
way round. It is the disruption in the libidinal bond with the
father which ipso facto results in a persisting need for attachment to the same sex, i.e. for the restoration of the disrupted
bond. It is the flight from the father that results in the pre-
dominance of a mother-attachment. However, precisely because
it is abnormal to be attached to the mother alone, the reparative
drive attempts to restore the balance, by re-establishing a
libidinal bond with the male. In a purely secondary sense, one
may speak of a flight from the mother, but this is not an attempt
to escape attachment to the mother as such. The attachment to
the mother, which is per se normal, is to be retained, but in
addition the attachment to the same sex is to be restored. What
the homosexual attempts to flee - quite rightly - is not the
mother, but the one-sidedness of an attachment to the mother
alone.

One might add at this point that this would also explain such
authority problems as the homosexual may experience vis-à-vis
the opposite sex. The primary authority problems are those
vis-à-vis the same sex, which are of their very nature expressive
of the defensive detachment which is central to the homosexual
phenomenon. However, we have seen that defensive detachment
from the same sex results in an undue prominence being given
to the remaining, otherwise normal, attachment to the opposite
sex. And, in the absence of a compensating bond with the same
sex, it is not surprising that this attachment to the opposite
sex should be experienced as oppressive, whether latently or
overtly. This may be marked by such attitudes as fear, resentment, defensiveness, or specific authority problems. However,

in contrast to the homosexual's primary authority problems, these secondary problems stem not from a defensive detachment (from the opposite sex) but from an abnormally isolated attachment. In this way it is proper to differentiate the two kinds of authority problems, since the underlying dynamics are by no means similar. It is true that the solution to both is the restoration of the capacity for attachment to the same sex. But same-sex authority problems directly require the resolution of same-sex detachment, whereas opposite-sex authority problems require no modification in the opposite-sex attachment as such, but only the restoration of the complementary attachment that has been missing.

Perhaps the most developed version of the theory of mother-fixation is that of Socarides (1968b) in his discussion of a case of male homosexuality of pre-oedipal origin. Here the fixation to the mother is traced back to 'the undifferentiated phase of the mother-child unity'. We would agree with this but only on the understanding that such a position is the consequence of radical same-sex disidentification. In the absence of such an understanding, the data must perforce be misinterpreted. Thus Socarides states:

> In his narcissistic object choice, the homosexual not only loves his partner as he himself wished to be loved by the mother, but reacts to him with sadistic aggression as once experienced towards the hostile mother for forcing separation.

On the contrary, it must be stated that both these emotions are genuinely and realistically directed towards the male, the father-figure, as a consequence of the disidentificatory trauma which - in its most radical form - is the genesis of the homosexual-paranoid position. It is separation from the father, not from the mother, that is central to the aetiology of male homosexuality. The male homosexual is seeking for lost love-objects, but this is not to be equated with an attempt to return to the mother-child symbiosis, since it is precisely this position that has already been forced on the homosexual - a fortiori the transsexual - as a result of the loss of the bond with the father. Socarides states that in male homosexuality 'there is an extremely strong fixation on the mother which cannot be dealt with.' This is hardly surprising, since it is not the bond with the mother that is problematic, but the absence of a comparable and complementary bond with the father. Nor is it surprising that this 'mother-fixation' should further involve a 'fixation on one's own sex'. This is but the reparative attempt to restore the bond that was disrupted by the defensive detachment from the same-sex love-source. On this understanding, it is misleading to say, 'The obligatory homosexual has been unable to make the progression from the mother-child unity of earliest infancy to individuation', or, 'He has failed to make the separation from the mother at the proper stage of development.' Both of these statements of

Socarides may be understood as descriptive of the consequences
of same-sex disidentification. But neither is to be understood
as a statement of the causation of homosexuality, as Socarides's
position would seem to imply. When the father-son bond has been
disrupted, only the mother-son bond is left. However, it is not
the mother-son bond that is the problem, but the absence of
the father-son bond. This has to be reiterated, since the point
is so centrally important, and yet it has been so completely
misunderstood hitherto. Moreover, the definition of the problem
also vitally affects the definition of the desired solution. If the
mother-son bond is seen as problematic in itself, it may be
considered desirable to weaken this attachment. However, the
loss of one attachment can hardly be compensated for by the loss
of the other attachment in addition. If such an attempt were
truly successful, it is likely that the consequences would be
harmful, if not actually catastrophic. Ideally, the growing child
should have a bond with each of his parents. But if two bonds
are better than one, one bond is certainly far better than none,
and hence it is vital not to attempt to disrupt such an attachment. The therapeutic goal must be seen as the overcoming of
the defensive detachment and the restoration of the missing
attachment. It is the capacity for relationship with the same sex,
rather than with the opposite sex, that must be the focus of
attention.

The attempt to restore the disrupted libidinal bond does in
fact constantly take place. The capacity for a homosexual love-
response is itself the reparative attempt, towards restoration
of the normal process of growth which has - abnormally - been
interrupted and left unfulfilled. Most importantly, this implies
that the homosexual response is not itself a problem, but rather
the attempted solution of an underlying problem. The problem
is the disruption of the child's libidinal bond with the parent of
the same sex, i.e. a defensive detachment from the love-source,
which subsequently prevents the fulfilment of the libidinal and
identificatory needs that are normally fulfilled through such an
attachment. The homosexual response aims at restoring and
completing this process of growth, the end result of which is
indeed heterosexuality, since heterosexuality merely implies the
capacity for relating to members of the opposite sex as a psychologically complete member of one's own sex.

It may be asked at this point why, if the homosexual response
is essentially reparative, does the reparative process so rarely
attain completion? Or, in other words, why does the homosexual,
on fulfilment of his needs for a same-sex attachment, not become
heterosexual? The answer is that in fact such needs are only
rarely fulfilled. In theory, they could and should be fulfilled,
and in practice it may be that they have been fulfilled more often
than is known. But there are major difficulties which militate
against such fulfilment. The chief of these is the persistence of
the negative side of the ambivalence. The defensive detachment
from the love-source may emerge from repression and thwart the

renewed attempt at attachment, i.e. disrupt the relationship. This is the central difficulty, which is inherent in the very nature of the homosexual phenomenon. After all, if it had not been for this defensive detachment from the love-source, the person would not have 'become homosexual' in the first place.

Another difficulty is the fact that in a homosexual relationship both partners have similar needs, and thus each is trying to meet his own needs through another person in whom there is a similar lack of fulfilment. In addition, if in one or both partners there are very marked dependency needs, it is possible that the relationship may never go sufficiently deep to meet these needs. In all cases some length of time is required for the fulfilment of same-sex libidinal needs, and in these cases most particularly. But more will be said later about these deep dependency needs.

Bearing in mind these qualifications, we shall here discuss how the reparative attempt works out in practice. The male homosexual's longing for masculine love is in fact a desire to attain masculinity - to restore and complete the same-sex identificatory process that had been thwarted in greater or lesser degree. Nunberg (1938) discusses the male homosexual's craving for big, strong men as partners. He speaks of this as 'sympathetic magic'. The homosexual believes that he may absorb strength through contact with a man of strength and thus, through contact with masculine men, become masculine himself. We would state that this is not quasi-magical, but the accurate realisation that the identificatory process takes place through the medium of a libidinal bond; and that, once disrupted, this process requires to be restored.

Bychowski (1945) speaks of the homosexual's sense of loss of virility and the consequent search for virility outside his own self. Unfortunately, Bychowski links this with feminine identification, rather than with masculine disidentification. He mentions the possibility of a defective father-identification in some cases, but this is seen as subordinate rather than central, and certainly not as the essential dynamic. Fenichel (1945a) likewise maintains the centrality of a mother-fixation, though his description of the desire for masculinity would be more congruous with our hypothesis of disidentification:[14]

> The passive submission to the father covers the unconscious idea of robbing him of his masculinity. 'Feminine' men often have not entirely given up their striving to be masculine. Unconsciously, they regard their femininity as temporary, as a means to an end; they regard the condition of being a masculine man's 'feminine' partner as learning the secrets of masculinity from the 'master', or as depriving him of those secrets. In such cases, the passive submission to the father is combined with traits of an old and original (oral) identification love of the father.

It is this last sentence that gives the key to the whole process.
The striving for masculinity in the context of a libidinal bond is
itself the renewal of the identificatory process that was once
disrupted by disidentification from the father. Examples of cases
where this striving is notably prominent may be found in Henry
(1950), who instances inter alia homosexuals wanting virile men
for partners, and passive relationships to older men (i.e.
father substitutes) or to very masculine persons. In other cases,
this underlying dynamic may not be so prominent, but we would
wish to postulate that it is generally applicable: in all cases, the
phenomenon is one of same-sex disidentification and the compen-
satory striving for renewal of the identificatory bond.

A number of writers mention the desire for the acquisition of
masculinity. Bieber et al. (1962) speak of the search for male
qualities.[15] The search for a large penis is partly for reasons of
symbolic incorporation, which in turn implies identification with
the powerful male. Ovesey et al. (1963) discuss the dependency
needs of the homosexual. The incorporation of the penis is the
way in which the dependent male undoes his castration and
through which 'masculine' strength become available to him.
Socarides (1968b) states that 'the homosexual makes an identification with the masculinity of his partner in the sexual act.'
When feeling weak, the homosexual wants a 'shot' of masculinity,
and thus masculinity is achieved through identification with the
partner's penis. The man chosen as a partner represents one's
forfeited masculinity regained. Socarides further states:

> He has not given up his maleness at all; he urgently and
> desperately wants to be a man, but is able to do this only
> by transiently identifying with the masculinity and penis of
> his partner in the sexual act.

It is true that the male homosexual has not 'given up' his
maleness, but this is only because he has not yet fully attained
it in the first place. He seeks to gain not what he has had but
has lost or given up; but what he has not yet attained. And if
the libidinal bond could be both fully restored, and maintained
uninterruptedly, the completion of the masculine identificatory
process could be attained.

Socarides later (1972) reiterates the interpretation of the homosexual act as the seeking of a 'shot' of masculinity. At the same
time, he asserts that it has been shown clinically that all male
homosexuals yearn to be men, rather than women, as commonly
supposed. We would agree that the reparative yearning of
homosexuals is for the restoration of the same-sex identificatory
process, i.e. to 'become men'. But we would also assert that
this yearning is only truly understood on a presupposition of
same-sex disidentification. It may not properly be linked as
Socarides attempts to do - with the so-called mother-fixation
that is itself a consequence of same-sex disidentification. Moreover, precisely because of disidentification, it is true to say

there is in some homosexuals a sense of femininity or an actual
longing to be women, which is essentially an aversive anti-
masculinity. It is not a mutually exclusive question of homosexuals either wanting to be women or wanting to be men. This
is a false dichotomy, based on a lack of appreciation of disidentification and its twofold implications. Because of disidentification,
there is in homosexuals both an aversive desire not to be men,
i.e. to be 'women', and a reparative desire for the restoration
of same-sex identification, i.e. to be men.

In this discussion we have covered the various aspects of the
phenomenon of same-sex ambivalence, stemming from gender
disidentification. This is the condition commonly referred to as
homosexuality or, in its most extreme form, transsexualism. It
has been demonstrated to be essentially a problem in the capacity
for relating to the same sex, rather than to the opposite sex.
And the correct definition of the problem must in turn affect the
definition of its resolution. The problem is of a twofold nature:
a defensive barrier against the love-source of the same sex and
the consequent lack of fulfilment of the libidinal and identificatory
needs that are normally fulfilled through the medium of such an
attachment. The resolution of the problem must involve both the
undoing of the defensive detachment and the fulfilling of needs
left unmet hitherto. The homosexual love-response is itself the
reparative attempt towards the meeting of unmet needs. However,
although such needs may often begin to be met while the defensive barrier persists in a state of repression, they may never be
completely met until the defensive detachment itself is resolved.
Nunberg (1938) speaks of the aim of homosexuality as a com-
promise between aggressive and libidinal impulses. It would be
truer to say that the reparative attempt towards libidinal attachment may at any time be thwarted by the resurgence of the
defensive detachment from the love-source. Bergler (1961)
states that homosexuality is not a drive, but a defence mechanism.
Rather, it is both. There is indeed a defence mechanism, and it
is directed towards the love-source of the same sex, not the
opposite sex. At the same time, there is a drive, whether overt
or repressed, towards the restoration of the disrupted attachment. The defence and the positive drive are to be correlated
with each other, and both alike operate in relation to the love-
source of the same sex.
    The so-called mother-fixation of the male homosexual is to be
interpreted as a flight from the father, and only consequentially
as a flight to the mother. Where male and female co-therapists
work together with male homosexuals, they provide a concrete
representation of the parental dyad which may make this pattern
of flight more evident and accessible. It is vital that this should
not be misinterpreted. Apparent flight to the mother is not
evidence of heterosexuality, but marks a continuing inability to
fulfil same-sex needs. It is an essentially pre-heterosexual
position, in that the flight from the father implies that the same-

sex identificatory process is still in some degree incomplete. It is the detachment from the father, not the attachment to the mother, that requires to be resolved. In the transsexual, this flight from the father is so radical and so deeply embedded that it manifests itself in an apparent cross-gender identity. In lesser degrees of disidentification, there may be a viable sense of masculine identity, but the flight from the same sex may be acted out in terms of authority problems or the disruption of libidinal attachments.

It would not therefore be true to speak of homosexuality as a flight from heterosexuality. This would be to miss the central point, viz. the defect in the relational capacity vis-à-vis the same sex. Bieber et al. (1962) speak of a fear of heterosexuality, but the detailed evidence they present is in fact entirely supportive of the theory of gender disidentification, as we have already pointed out. Socarides (1968b) says that the homosexual runs from all women in order to resolve the separation from the mother. We must rather say that the homosexual both runs from and seeks for men, in consequence of and in order to resolve detachment from the father.

The homosexual does not renounce heterosexuality: rather, he has not yet attained it. Bieber et al. (1962) declare that continued fear of heterosexuality in the adult homosexual is inappropriate to his current reality.[16] On the contrary, we must state that the non-practice of heterosexuality is entirely appropriate to the reality of his psychological make-up. It is unrealistic to expect heterosexual behaviour, unless of a more or less superficial nature, where there is not yet an underlying heteropsychologic personality structure. Until the same-sex identificatory process is complete, i.e. until homosexual needs have been met, there is no basis for a truly heterosexual response. Once a person has become a psychologically complete member of his own sex, he is by definition able to respond heterosexually, i.e. as a full member of one sex towards a member of the other sex. The fulfilment of homosexual needs is the capacity for heterosexual response. It would be true to say that all homosexuals are potentially heterosexual, but genuine heterosexuality can only be attained by the fulfilment of homosexual needs, and most certainly not by the abrogation of such fulfilment, as is commonly supposed. To block the fulfilment of homosexual needs is to block the restoration of the normal process of growth. Or, in other words, to block the fulfilment of homosexual needs is to block the very path towards the attainment of heterosexuality.

5 THE FEMALE HOMOSEXUAL

The psychodynamic structure of homosexuality in the female is
analogous to that in the male, in that it too involves same-sex
ambivalence. Here too we shall be able to examine the various
components of this ambivalence. Although female homosexuality
has generally received less attention than male homosexuality,
it should become apparent that there is in fact ample material
for a comparable analysis of the female, and in some detail.

A defensive detachment from the same-sex love-source will be
marked by hostility, whether latent or overt, towards the mother
and towards other members of the same sex. This defensive
detachment implies a blocking of the normal identificatory process. The consequent absence of femininity, based on a defensive anti-femininity, may in more extreme cases manifest itself
in a sense of cross-gender identity, i.e. a quasi-masculine
identity, whether in the lesbian or in the female-to-male transsexual. However, both cross-dressing and an apparent identification with the father are to be interpreted in terms of this
defensive anti-femininity: apparent cross-gender identification
is a direct consequence of same-sex disidentification.

Moreover, since disidentification - especially in its more
radical forms - results in the missing out of a major part of
normal growth, we may expect to find some expression of this
incompletion. In fact we find much evidence of childishness;
marked dependency needs; jealousy and possessiveness; a sense
of inferiority; and depression, some suicidal thoughts and
attempts, and the phenomenon known as aphanisis or 'fear of
total extinction'.

However, in spite of the defensive detachment and its consequences, there is - as in men - a reparative drive towards
restoration of the broken libidinal attachment, and hence towards
fulfilment of the libidinal and identificatory needs that are
normally fulfilled through the medium of such an attachment.
Thus, the female homosexual seeks for female love, which is an
essentially maternal love. It is at times quite evident that the
lesbian is looking for mother substitutes, and many studies have
commented on the 'mother-daughter' character of the lesbian
relationship. This need for the mother is often misleadingly
interpreted as a mother-fixation, i.e. as an abnormal attachment.
But it would be more proper to interpret this as an abiding
need for attachment, consequent on actual detachment. In the
female as in the male, homosexuality marks a defect in the
capacity for relating to the same sex.

We may begin by reminding ourselves that the defensive detachment from the same-sex love-source is realistic in its origin.
Various writers (Caprio, 1960; Kenyon, 1968a; Barnhouse, 1977)
mention known difficulties in the mother-daughter relationship.
In a number of instances the difficulty may not be known,
whether because of lack of information or - significantly -
through an inability to recognise what is likely to result in a
defensive detachment in the child. This latter may be especially
true of the more radical forms of disidentification in early
infancy, i.e. the paranoid-homosexual condition. The pathological
mourning response to early separation (or to early hostile
behaviour, which - like separation - is detrimental to the infant's
capacity for attachment and hence results in a similar 'mourning'
response) has not hitherto been linked with long-term effects on
identity and on homo-emotional needs. For this reason, the
converse has also been true: homosexuality has either not been
linked with early trauma of this nature; or, if occasionally the
association has been made, the nature of the link has not in
fact been understood. What we are postulating is that female
homosexuality always stems from some actual difficulty in the
mother-child relationship, whether or not it is still possible to
identify this difficulty retrospectively. At the same time, we
would also assert that the difficulty may be either wilful or
involuntary on the mother's part. It is sometimes, but certainly
not always, deliberately bad behaviour by the mother that affects
her daughter's capacity for attachment to her.

Hostility towards the hurtful love-source is involved in this
defensive detachment; and, the more radical the disidentification,
the more severe is the degree of hostility that maintains it.
Deutsch (1932) speaks of a 'murderous hatred of the mother',
and Krafft-Ebing (1899) mentions an actual murder by a lesbian
of her lover. Such an instance is, unfortunately, not unique.
However, although all lesbianism presupposes some degree of
hostility, whether latent or overt, towards the love-source, not
all hostility is of this intensity.

Henry (1950) and Caprio (1960) speak of the aggressiveness
and ambivalence of the lesbian in her love relationships; and
Barnhouse (1977) mentions the more general aggressiveness of
the lesbian, which may - for instance - manifest itself in
antagonism towards more feminine colleagues at work. In both
instances the hostility is directed towards the same sex, i.e.
towards the potential or actual love-source. The negative side
of the ambivalence may re-emerge either in isolation or within
the context of a renewed libidinal attachment. West (1977)
reports that 'the explosively aggressive quality of lesbian loves
has been held to reflect the aggressive elements in the original
mother-daughter relationship.' We would agree with this, but
differ from the interpretation given. Hostile feelings do not
derive from the infant's sense of helpless dependency per se.
And 'murderous aggression towards the mother' is not to be
merely correlated with the fact that the mother can threaten

and punish as well as offer love. Unless such punishment is
markedly severe or involves withdrawal of the mother from her
child (i.e. separation), it is unlikely actually to terminate the
child's capacity for attachment to her mother, which is what we
are discussing here. Unpleasantness experienced within an on-
going relationship may arouse some degree of resentment, but it
is the actual severance of relationship that is involved in disidentification and that accounts for the emotion of severe hatred
(a pathological mourning response to the termination of attachment).

It has been the inability to interpret hatred as a realistic response to difficulties in early relationship that has been the chief
limitation of theoretical work hitherto. Jones (1927) states:

> The fundamental – and, so far as one can see, inborn – factors
> that are decisive . . . appear to be two – namely, an unusual
> intensity of oral erotism and of sadism respectively. These
> converge in an *intensification of the oral-sadistic stage*, which
> I would regard. . . as *the central characteristic of homosexual
> development in women.*

Such an account is descriptive rather than explanatory. Jones
is correct in observing the intensity of the two emotions of love
(oral erotism) and hate (sadism), but he assumes that they are
inborn and makes no attempt to explore possible precipitating
factors. He continues by asserting that the sadistic temperament
'is accompanied by a ready reversal of love to hate.' To assume
that such transformations 'just happen' in intrapsychic life is
unsatisfactory. It is more plausible to hypothesise that changes
and reversals in emotional states occur for some specific reason.
The whole thrust of the present study is in favour of this hypothesis. The two emotions of hate (defensive detachment) and love
(the persisting need for attachment) are specifically correlated
with early interpersonal trauma.

As a subsidiary point, one might add that it is the relative
strength of one or other side of this ambivalence that character-
ises the different types of lesbian. Jones mentions two groups.
Where 'sadism' is paramount, there is an interest in men and in
being accepted by men as one of themselves. Where 'oral erotism'
is paramount, there is little or no interest in men but the libido
focuses on women. We would suggest that this division of types
is more apparent than real. In all cases we would postulate an
underlying ambivalence. However, in the former group the
aversive side of the ambivalence is more prominent, i.e. the
flight from women and the apparent cross-gender interests.
In the latter group the reparative side of the ambivalence is
more in evidence, i.e. the drive towards restoration of attachment with women.

Deutsch (1932) discusses the emotions of hate and love in a
particular case of lesbianism. She links murderous hatred for
the mother with the mother's suppression of the patient's early

masturbation. We would not accept this particular correlation,
since it seems insufficient to account for the termination of
attachment, and at most suggests some displacement of emotion
from the fundamentally traumatic event. (It is quite possible
that, subsequent to detachment, the normal disciplinary activity
of the mother might evoke an abnormally strong response – but
this is quite different from suggesting that it is causative of
such detachment.) In any case, Deutsch effectively qualifies
her statement by commenting, 'The reaction of hatred towards
her mother was perceptible also in other situations of childhood
and was in accordance with the patient's sadistic constitution.'

We have already criticised this suggestion of an inherent
sadism not evoked by external events. Deutsch goes on to speak
of a guilt reaction to these feelings of hatred, which causes
their transformation into feelings of love. If this merely intrapsychic transformation were correlated with social reality, it
would be possible to speak of hatred as arising in response to
trauma and as repressing the capacity for attachment, so that
love-needs persist unmet.

It is possible to make a similar reassessment of Bergler (1961).
In addition to the 'injustice-collecting' that he regards as
characteristic of all homosexuals, Bergler speaks of a special
three-layer structure in female homosexuality: (a) masochistic
seeking of refusal by 'the Giantess and her successive repre-
sentatives', i.e. by the mother and by later mother-substitutes,
(b) defensive pseudo-hatred; (c) defensive pseudo-love.[2] Thus:[3]

> Her homosexuality was a defense against both her deeper
> masochistic attachment to her mother, and her more superficial
> – though also unconsciously determined – *pseudo-aggressive
> hatred* of her mother.

Homosexual love is but the final manoeuvre in this three-tiered
strategy. It states, 'I do not hate her, I love her sexually.'
This libidinous defence is unconscious and is transferred
secondarily from the mother to other women. Bergler reaches
these conclusions in answer to two questions which he poses to
the patient in question:[4] 'If you hate your mother so much,
how do you account for the fact that, sexually, you turn to a
woman?' And,[5] 'How do you account for the fact that you became
attracted to women when the first person who disappointed you
so deeply was a woman?'

Bergler assumes that the facts he draws attention to are contradictory. However, what we are dealing with is not a contradiction, but a paradox, which becomes explicable in terms of
disidentificatory ambivalence. Precisely because the mother was
hurtful, this elicited hatred and caused the daughter to repress
her capacity for attachment. The need for attachment has thus
persisted unmet, and the homosexual response is the attempt to
restore this attachment. Bergler comments that his patient could
not explain how her mother's brutality could account for her

homosexuality, and states that it is mistaken to assume a direct
connection between the two. On the present hypothesis, there
is no difficulty in making this connection; indeed some such
difficulty in the mother-daughter relationship is for us an
essential aetiological factor. At the same time, this would account
for the lesbian's tendency to construct situations in which she
is unjustly treated. This is not a merely unmotivated masochism,
but rather the attempt to replicate the early infantile situation
in which she had good reason for feeling unjustly treated.

To conclude our present discussion of Bergler, we may suggest
that it is a false dichotomy to designate lesbianism as an
aggressive rather than an erotic conflict.[6] This is to give undue
prominence to what is only one side of an overall ambivalence, in
which both libidinal and aggressive elements are properly
involved. Moreover, this ambivalence is not peculiar to female
homosexuality. It is, as we have already explained, the essential
characteristic of homosexuality in both genders.

Another theory we must reassess in the light of the disidentificatory hypothesis is that of Socarides (1968a). Here again there
is an overemphasis on one side of the ambivalence. Homosexuality
is stated to involve an aggressive conflict, in which the
aggression is secondarily libidinised.[7] The wish to love and be
loved is seen as a reaction formation and defence against
hatred,[8] rather than as the girl's normal capacity for attachment
that has been blocked by a defensive reaction to trauma. There
is little or no sense of hatred as a socially realistic response.
'Intense sadistic feelings' and 'murderous fantasies' towards the
mother are mentioned, but are said to arise from pre-oedipal
fears.[9]

> Is the accentuation of sadism from the primal scene or is there
> congenital predisposition? Is it perhaps due to early weaning
> or that the primal scene was experienced during the period of
> acute oral frustration and in conjunction with it?[10]

The conflict is seen as stemming from the young child's
aggressive and destructive impulses towards her mother and the
resultant defences against these impulses, i.e. the conflict is
defined as purely intrapsychic rather than as a truly interpersonal conflict with intrapsychic repercussions. The lesbian
is stated to be afraid of her own oral aggressive desires towards
her mother.[11] Instead of actual trauma from the love-source,
Socarides speaks of the 'assumed murderous impulses of the
mother'.[12] The lesbian is said to project her own fear and hatred
on to her mother.[13] The mother denied her the male organ as a
punishment, especially for masturbation. We have already
criticised this latter view in connection with Deutsch. Here we
may add that the plausibility of this view may be due in part
to the role played by masturbation in lesbian practices. On our
own hypothesis, this is to be regarded as the secondary eroticisation of a condition that is not essentially erotic. Socarides,

however, ascribes a more central role to this eroticisation:[14]

> Invariably present is an intense conflict over masturbation
> which began early in childhood. In the homosexual act 'mother'
> is sanctioning masturbation through a sharing of the guilt
> mechanism.

This is to misinterpret lesbianism as the reassertion of
suppressed sexual activity, whereas in fact it is the restoration
of a broken attachment (which may, secondarily, be eroticised,
but need not be thus expressed at all). Even on Socarides's
account, lesbian activity does not provide a solution to early
conflict, since such activity may 'awaken severe sadistic
impulses'.[15] Or, in other words, the negative side of the ambivalence may re-emerge within the context of a renewed libidinal
attachment, and may well disrupt it again. This does not imply
that homosexual love is itself sadistic, but rather that the normal
capacity for same-sex attachment may repeatedly be thwarted
by the re-emergence of the persisting defensive barrier against
the love-source.

At this point, we may turn to consider some further implications
of this defensive anti-femininity. Henry (1950) speaks of homosexuality as an expression of rebellion against being a female,[16]
but such a statement as this is likely to be misinterpreted. Due
to the interruption of the normal identificatory process, psycho
logical femininity has remained to a greater or lesser degree
incomplete in the lesbian. The lesbian cannot 'rebel' against
being something which she is not in the first place. What is
involved in lesbianism is an ambivalence to the same-sex love-
source, through an attachment to which one becomes a psychologically complete member of one's own anatomic sex. It is this
that we are referring to when we speak of a defensive anti-
femininity. The defence is not against a state already achieved,
but against the means through which such a state may be
achieved. It is vital to note this difference in emphasis.

Jones (1927) speaks of an identification with the father in
female homosexuality, which represents a denial of femininity.
This marks a confusion of cause and effect. It is the disidentification from the mother (= 'a denial of femininity') which results
in an apparent identification with the father. Socarides (1963)
likewise speaks of how identification with the father keeps
feminine wishes repressed. The lesbian in effect asserts, 'I
cannot possibly desire a man's penis for my gratification, since
I already possess one of my own, or at all events I want nothing
else than one of my own.' However, it is meaningless to speak
of the wishes of mature femininity being repressed, when mature
femininity itself has not been attained. The essential 'feminine
wishes' involved in lesbianism are the desire for a libidinal
attachment to the female (mother), i.e. the desire for the medium
through which a mature feminine identity may be attained. However, the repression of this 'feminine wish' and an apparent

cross-gender identification are both alike the results of same-sex disidentification.

Moreover, when identification with the father - rather than disidentification from the mother - is assumed to be primary, it becomes difficult to account for the lesbian's love of women. Fenichel (1945a) speaks of a desire to love the mother in the way the father loved her. Socarides (1968a) suggests that lesbians may choose women who represent themselves and love them as they would wish to have been loved by the father. In either case, lesbian love is seen as something abnormal. In contrast, we would see the lesbian's love for women as the restoration of the girl's normal attachment to her mother, which was - abnormally - disrupted. It is not a quasi-masculine love, but a genuinely feminine, identificatory love.

Granted this, it becomes fair to speak - secondarily - of an apparent cross-gender identity resulting from same-sex disidentification. In its extreme form. this may manifest itself as transsexualism. However, we have indicated that there is little to distinguish this psychodynamically from the most radical form of homosexuality, and in the female there is often little overt difference between the two as well. It is unfortunate that little attention has been paid to the phenomenon of female cross-dressing. The masculine appearance of some lesbians has become part of the popular stereotype, but has received insufficient serious investigation. Fenichel (1945a) makes the chief theoretical contribution:[17]

> 'Making believe that one possesses a penis' and 'playing father' are the unconscious meanings of female transvestitism. . . . Transvestitism in women is a displacement of the envy of the penis to an envy of masculine appearance.

This comment is reiterated by Lukianowicz (1959b), who adds that, since transvestism is a symbolic denial of castration, there is no place for female transvestites. Since 'transvestism' means, etymologically, 'cross-dressing', it is perhaps unfair to restrict the term to one particular manifestation of the more general phenomenon. This very restriction may account for the relative lack of attention paid to female cross-dressing. Cross-dressing may have various meanings, not just one. In the female, cross-dressing is to be linked directly with disidentification. It is not a matter of wishing to identify with the father or envy of masculinity, but the consequence of an aversive anti-femininity. We would allow that secondarily there may perhaps be some genuine though superficial cross-gender identification, but this is to be seen entirely as a consequence of same-sex disidentification, in the absence of which it could not occur.

Krafft-Ebing (1899) and Henry (1950) detail cases of apparent cross-gender behaviour in women. The disidentified female may be boyish in dress and attitude, may wish to be a male or even feel 'herself' to be a male. However, just as disidentification may occur in either gender, so disidentificatory cross-dressing may occur in the male as well as in the female. This study does not undertake to discuss male transvestism, as more narrowly defined. But it is relevant to note here that the disidentificatory cross-dressing of the male transsexual is not the symbolic denial of castration, but its opposite: it is the expression of the psychological castration that is involved in radical disidentification from the male.

Apparent masculinity in the female implies the disruption of an attachment to the mother. The normal attachment to the father thus remains, abnormally, as the only channel for attachment. This remaining attachment may of itself be good or poor. Bene (1965b) emphasises the significance of a poor father-daughter relationship for female homosexuality; but in specifically suggesting that the mother-daughter relationship is less important, this would seem to be yet another instance of confusion of cause and effect. Kenyon (1968a) notes that many lesbians have had poor parental relationships, whether with their mothers or their fathers, but does not suggest what may underlie this. The lesbian may sometimes also show hostility to men in general (Fenichel, 1945a). Two reasons may be suggested for this hostility to the male. Firstly, it may arise in reaction to the abnormality of being capable of only masculine attachment. Disidentification may have rendered same-sex attachment impossible, but it does not for that reason make an abnormally isolated cross-gender attachment entirely palatable. Secondly, since the disidentified female usually remains female to appearances, difficulties may arise in relationships with the father and other members of the opposite sex. The lesbian may resent being treated as female, and other persons may resent the lesbian not living up to feminine expectations. Hence, it is hardly surprising that difficulties should arise, but these are a consequence of disidentification and not its cause.

Finally, it may be noted that the father-daughter relationship for the disidentified female is not as intense as the mother-son relationship for the disidentified male. West (1977) makes this point about the lesbian,[18] and Pauly (1969) makes a similar comment about the female-to-male transsexual.[19] Although it is not entirely clear why this should be the case, one may tentatively link this with the different position of the boy and the girl vis-à-vis the first object, viz. the mother. Disidentification for the boy implies regression to attachment to the first love-source, and this may account for the relative strength of the so-called mother-fixation consequent on disidentification. However, in the case of the girl, disidentification implies a more radical loss, in that the first love-source is lost, and the girl cannot regress to a father-attachment but must progress to it. The disidentified boy reverts to an old attachment, but the disidentified girl must move on to a new attachment. It is possible that this may account for the subsequent difference in intensity of relationships with the parent of the opposite anatomic sex.

The childishness of the radically disidentified person is another feature that deserves comment, and one which may manifest itself in a variety of ways. We shall discuss this in connection with the female, but our remarks are to be taken to refer to disidentified persons of both genders. The first and most important point to note is that this childishness is essentially realistic. If a normal channel of attachment has remained blocked since early infancy, the person in question is - in certain important respects - a psychological child. This is not to deny that such persons may attain physiological and intellectual maturity and, at least to appearances, some kind of social maturity. But otherwise their state is one of radically incomplete psychological growth.

Storr (1964) speaks of how the lesbian may demand the kind of love and attention 'which a child of three or less may justifiably demand from its mother'.[20] For the present writer, this was one of the most important clues with which this investigation began. If someone behaves like a child of two or three, might this not imply that they genuinely still have the actual needs of a child of that age, and that something occurred at that age to prevent further maturation? The evidence gathered in this study would seem to confirm this hypothesis.

In the case of the female, there is even an actual case history available, which illustrates how separation trauma may result in disidentification. This is the story of Laura (Bowlby, Robertson and Rosenbluth, 1952). A study - including a film - were made at the time of Laura's visit to hospital for eight days at age two-and-a-half. A contrast was noted between Laura's expressed desire for her mother and her inability to greet her when she did come to visit. Moreover, the separation was repeated for a longer period only four months later, when the mother was in hospital for four weeks while having a baby. For two days after this, Laura did not seem to recognise her mother - she was friendly, but detached in attitude. This second separation would seem to have reinforced the effect of the first, but the first alone was clearly traumatic. Some months after her stay in hospital, Laura happened to see the film, which her parents were watching. At the sight of this, Laura cried out, 'Where *was* you, Mummy? Where *was* you?' *And she turned from her mother to her father*.[21] A clearer illustration of the disidentificatory process could not be asked for. It is only unfortunate that there is no information available about Laura's subsequent development. It is, of course, possible that in this instance the trauma may in fact have been wholly or partially resolved in childhood, or that it may have remained repressed and not (yet) become overt in the adult. But the given evidence suggests that Laura did undergo precisely the process we have been discussing.

The perpetuation of childishness is due to the disruption, in early childhood, of the girl's normal and necessary attachment to her mother. It is thus hardly surprising that the lesbian relationship, in which this broken attachment is restored, may take on the character of a mother-child relationship. The child-ishness of the radically disidentified female may be particularly striking. Storr (1964) comments:[22]

> This particular woman needed the kind of mothering which is only given to small babies. She needed to feel that, for a time, her requirements were paramount, so that, if she wanted attention from her mother-substitute, the latter should at once abandon every other pursuit and rush to her side. Moreover, she was unable to tolerate any kind of attention being given to anyone else, and would fly into violent rages in which she attacked the mother-substitute physically if she believed that her place was being usurped by another.

We may compare this with Simon's description (1967) of a female-to-male transsexual:

> In this patient, masculine attitudes are consistently belied by infantile behavior in relation to her huge, maternal partner. When frustrated, she becomes hopelessly angered, manifesting an incredible childlike appearance with petulant looks, pouting lips, and clenched fists. In turn, immediate maternal caresses are elicited from the partner. This observable sequence is a remarkable caricature of a mother-child relationship.

In each of these instances the childishness has become apparent within the context of a restored attachment. It is quite possible that such childishness may not always be apparent. When there is no attachment or only a relatively superficial attachment (i.e. one in which the full extent of dependency needs is not realised), there may sometimes be little or no overt childishness. Moreover, even within the context of a deep, restored attachment, the childishness may become apparent chiefly when the person is thwarted. Otherwise, it should be possible for the person to function notably better than previously, since at last the missing channel for growth has been restored. We might note in passing that Walinder's comments (1967) on psycho-infantilism do not seem sufficiently specific to delineate the kind of childishness we are discussing here. As it is, Walinder reaches the conclusion that 50 per cent of transsexual men, i.e. eighteen in the given study, show signs of being psycho-infantile, but only two of the transsexual women.[23] On the present hypothesis, all trans-sexuals - whether male or female - must by definition be psycho-infantile, but some may show it less than others.

Jealousy and possessiveness are two characteristics which are (a) childish, in that they relate directly to actual deprivation in childhood; (b) only likely to become apparent within the context of a fairly deep renewed attachment. Possessiveness marks the urgent desire to retain the restored attachment - an attachment that is so much needed and that has for so long remained unful-

filled. Jealousy likewise stems from the fear of renewed loss or
deprivation. The literature contains frequent references to these
characteristics, e.g. Caprio (1960), Storr (1964). Barnhouse
(1977). Jealousy is likely to involve hostility towards the love-
source, and thus may link with the re-emergence of the negative
side of the ambivalence. Krafft-Ebing (1899) speaks of violent
jealousy in lesbian love, and even murder, as does Caprio (1960).
The hatred that may sometimes fully re-emerge in the disidentified
indicates how great a hurt was involved in the trauma of disidentification. In the majority of instances, it would seem that the
repressed hurt and hate never re-emerge so fully as to be acted
out in this way. But even in the absence of acting out, the situation is one of human tragedy, and social disturbance is only an
end-product of this long-standing tragedy.

Another characteristic is a sense of inferiority. Socarides
(1968a) speaks specifically of 'a deep sense of inferiority'.[24]
Not all feelings of inferiority are the correlate of disidentification,
but where disidentification has occurred a marked sense of
inferiority - whether fully conscious or not - is its correlate.
The sense of personal worth which the child normally receives
from its parents' love, cannot be received if the child's capacity
for attachment has been repressed consequent on trauma.
Whether or not love is offered, it can no longer be received. And
if love cannot be received, then neither can a sense of worth.
The resultant state may be designated 'inferiority' (Socarides,
1968a) or 'masochism' (Bergler, 1961). Whatever the label, it is
important to note its socially realistic referents: intrapsychic
damage is a consequence of early interpersonal difficulties.

Alternatively, the sense of loss consequent on defensive
detachment may manifest itself in a state of depression. This is
of quite frequent occurrence in the lesbian (Kenyon, 1968a,
1970; Saghir et al. 1970b), and in the female-to-male transsexual
(Walinder, 1967). Suicidal thoughts or attempts may occur
(Caprio, 1960; Walinder, 1967; Socarides, 1968a). Saghir et al.
(1970b) estimate that as many as 23 per cent of homosexual
women may attempt suicide.

Since the loss is one of attachment, the restoration of attachment may result in the lifting of depression; and, conversely,
the dissolution of an attachment - which implies a renewal of the
loss - may result in depression or some other manifestation of
response to loss. Deutsch (1932) details the case of a woman
whose suicidal depression disappeared when an overtly lesbian
relationship was established. This is hardly surprising. The
loss underlying the depression was one of attachment to the
mother, and the loss began to be made good within the renewed
attachment provided by the lesbian relationship. On the other
hand, the break-up of a relationship will often precipitate
depression (Saghir et al., 1970b). In its most extreme form,
this renewed sense of loss is known as 'aphanisis' (Jones, 1927).
This is misinterpreted as being 'the total extinction of the
capacity for sexual enjoyment'. It is non-sexual, though it is

linked with the radical diversion of the growth of gender
identity from its normal channels. Aphanisis marks the sheer
sense of loss experienced in disidentification. In the adult it is
the replication of the feelings of the infant who has 'lost her
mother', i.e. has lost the capacity for attachment to her mother.
The sense of loss in the adult is entirely realistic, in that the
loss has persisted since childhood and has not yet been made
up for. Aphanisis may occur on the loss of a love-object, or if
in the course of therapy it is attempted to separate the lesbian
from her partner (Socarides, 1968a). Any such attempt must be
utterly counter-therapeutic, since the lesbian relationship is
itself the reparative attempt to restore missing growth through
a restored attachment. The attachment is not the problem, but
the attempt to solve the problem (of missing growth). Disruption
of the attachment can only renew the problem and not resolve
it.

Depression and aphanisis may occur when a restored attachment is terminated. Both of these responses mark the sheer
sense of loss itself. Alternatively, renewed loss may bring
renewed anger for loss. Hastings (1941) mentions a lesbian who
showed paranoid manifestations whenever her homosexual
relationships broke up. However, when relationships are terminated by external circumstances, the negative side of the
ambivalence need not always become apparent, unless it was
already close to re-emergence from repression. What happens
more commonly is that the relationship is disrupted from within,
with the negative side of the ambivalence itself causing the disruption. The perennial problem of the homosexual ambivalence
is that the reparative attempt may at any time be thwarted by
the re-emergence of the defensive barrier. There is a tendency
towards renewal of loss, through renewal of detachment, that
is inherent in the very structure of the homosexual phenomenon.

A major consequence of defensive detachment is that dependency needs remain unmet. The meeting of such needs would of
itself imply the meeting of libidinal and identificatory needs.
Thus, so long as dependency needs remain unmet, the needs to
receive love from and identify with the parent of the same sex
cannot be met. Barnhouse (1977) speaks of unsatisfied dependency needs as connected with inadequate mothering in childhood.[25]
Unfortunately, she immediately negates this insight by stating
that 'the homosexual adaptation in such cases is essentially a
regressive attempt to secure the safety and pleasure of identification with the maternal principle.'[26] In fact, the logical corollary
of her former statement is that the homosexual adaptation is
essentially the attempt to meet unmet needs. It is not unresolved
mother dependency that is at issue, but rather unfulfilled mother
dependency. Moreover, the attempt to meet such needs cannot
fairly be termed regressive, since to meet these needs of itself
promotes further growth. However, missing growth will not be
restored if we assume that there has not been any growth missed
out on in the first place. We may not speak of regression to a

certain point when progress (growth) from that point has not yet taken place.

In order to meet the problem of missing growth consequent on detachment, the lesbian seeks a renewed attachment. This is essentially a search for a mother substitute, whether or not the lesbian is aware of this. The overtly 'mother-daughter' character of many lesbian relationships is a commonplace of the psychiatric literature (Freud, 1933 [1932]; Deutsch, 1932; Fenichel, 1945a; Henry, 1950; Caprio, 1960; Bergler, 1961; Storr, 1964; Socarides, 1963, 1968a). In connection with this, it is often suggested that a mother-fixation is significant in the aetiology of female homosexuality (Jones, 1927; Fenichel, 1945a; Caprio, 1960; Bergler, 1961; Socarides, 1968a; West, 1977). The apparent mother fixation marks, not a persisting attachment, but a persisting need for attachment, consequent on actual detachment. The term 'fixation' is misleading in that it tends to mask the true nature of the problem. Moreover, it may lead to the assertion that the lesbian's need is for separation from the mother (Socarides, 1968a; Barnhouse, 1977). Such separation is, of course, the very problem of lesbianism, and most emphatically not its solution.

Barnhouse (1977) states that basic gender identity for both boys and girls depends on separation from the mother.[27] This must be denied. While proper for the normal growth of boys, such a process is pathological for girls and detrimental to the development of a feminine identity. Likewise, to state that the father is necessarily other to the girl, however tangled the relationship with him, is to beg the question.[28] The father should indeed be other, but when disidentification from the mother has occurred, the girl has only a father-attachment left, and this necessarily reduces the normal sense of otherness in the relationship. Barnhouse further states that a pathologically close mother-child relationship cannot affect a girl's sense of femininity, and hence that true transsexualism is unknown in women.[29] Her premise is correct, but her conclusion is mistaken. Transsexualism is caused by disidentification from the parent of the same sex. In the boy, an abnormal intensity in the otherwise normal mother-attachment is the result of this. In the girl, however, transsexualism stems from an unresolved disruption in the mother-child relationship. True transsexualism is certainly to be found in the anatomic female as well as in the anatomic male.

It is often suggested that a mother who values her own femininity is important as a model for identification (Storr, 1964; Barnhouse, 1977). Stoller (1972) actually states that a feminine and heterosexual mother is needed for the girl to become feminine and heterosexual. This is to misunderstand the nature of the identificatory process. It is not the availability of models, but the capacity for relating to such models, that is crucial. Whether models are good or bad in themselves is strictly irrelevant when disidentification has occurred, since the capacity for relationship has itself been repressed. The fundamental requirement for same-sex identification is an uninterrupted attachment to a figure of the same sex. This attachment is of itself identificatory. External modelling can be only superficial in the absence of such an attachment. And in the context of such an attachment, external modelling may be good or poor but cannot contradict the fundamental sense of identity that is being received through the attachment itself. The interruption of a relationship with a mother – whether she is heterosexual or homosexual – is certainly pathological. Conversely, an uninterrupted relationship will itself guarantee basic gender identity, even if the mother is herself homosexual rather than heterosexual.

It is not the mother's self-image or her attitude towards her daughter's gender role that affects the daughter's femininity, but the daughter's own capacity for relationship to her mother. Similarly, the father's attitude becomes irrelevant if disidentification has taken place. Socarides (1969) sees it as important that the father should accept his daughter's femininity. A father's acceptance may reinforce his daughter's femininity if the girl is attached to her mother, but such acceptance can do nothing to promote femininity in the absence of a mother-attachment. Thus, we must also disagree with Bacon (1965),[30] who states that a woman with a good relationship with one parent will not develop overt homosexuality. If that parent is the mother, there will be no homosexual development in the first place. But if that parent is the father, and the mother-attachment has actually been disrupted, there is certainly at least latent homosexuality. And, however deeply repressed, there is always the possibility of the latent becoming overt. No cross-gender attachment, however good, can ever make up for a missing same-sex attachment.

The hypothesis of disidentification implies an environmental rather than biological aetiology for the conditions of homosexuality and transsexualism. However, this does not imply that all the children in a given family should be similarly affected. A general similarity of environment is not the point at issue, but rather a specific (and often unintentional) trauma to one child or – sometimes – to more than one child. The fact that a lesbian or female transsexual may have a feminine and heterosexual sister (Bergler, 1961; Pauly, 1969) is not in any way remarkable.

Since homosexuality and transsexualism are essentially disorders in the capacity for relating to the same sex, it is improper to define them in terms of repulsion from or fear of heterosexuality (Fenichel, 1945a; Barnhouse, 1977). To speak of renouncing mature heterosexuality (Bacon, 1965) or abandoning the heterosexual position (Socarides, 1968a) is illogical. One cannot renounce or abandon what one has never yet attained. Bacon (1965) actually perpetuates popular misconceptions by defining homosexuality as 'the perversion or turning away of instincts from their normal heterosexual channels into other channels.'[31] This is incorrect. Heterosexuality has not yet been

attained – and will never be truly attained *unless and until*
'homosexual' needs have been met. Barnhouse (1977) states that
no woman who is properly related to her contrasexual component
ever becomes homosexual.[33] This again misdefines the issue. It
is the woman who is properly related to her 'homosexual' component who never becomes homosexual, since the fulfilment of
homosexual needs itself implies the attainment of heterosexuality.
The adult homosexual is, paradoxically, a person in whom homosexual needs have not been met and in whom they still remain
to be met.

At the conclusion of her study, Barnhouse states that
homosexuality may provide some satisfaction, but does not mark
the achievement of the goal of completeness.[34] This is true, but
not in quite the sense that Barnhouse intends. Homosexuality
is marked by incompletion, i.e. the absence of some degree of
normal growth, so the homosexual cannot – unless superficially –
act as if growth has been completed. But homosexuality involves
both a state of incompletion and also a striving for completion.
The homosexual response is itself the reparative attempt towards
completion. It is not enough to acknowledge that homosexuality
involves incompletion. It must also be recognised that completion
cannot be attained without the fulfilment of homosexual needs.
Homosexuality may not be the goal of human growth, but it is
certainly the normal, and indeed only, means towards the goal.

6 TOWARDS THE HEALING OF THE DEEPLY WOUNDED

For a problem to be solved, it must first be clear what the nature of the problem is. The solution, and the means used toward the solution, depend on how the problem is defined at the outset. This may sound like a statement of the obvious, but we would wish to assert that it is precisely this consideration that has been neglected and hence has led to confusion. In connection with this, two particular conclusions arise from this study. First, that homosexuality essentially involves a defect in the capacity for relating to the same sex - not the opposite sex, as is commonly assumed. To define homosexuality as same-sex love is misleading, not because this definition is untrue per se, but - significantly - because it is only partially true (and therefore, taken in isolation, is partially untrue). The whole truth of homosexuality is that it is a phenomenon of same-sex ambivalence. It is this difficulty that needs to be tackled and met.

Second, homosexual love (one side of the homosexual ambivalence) is not itself the problem at issue, but rather the means toward the solution of the problem. The underlying problem is a twofold one. There is a defensive detachment from the love-source. And, in consequence of this, needs for love, dependency and identification which are normally met through the medium of such an attachment, remain unmet. Since the problem is one of a disruption in attachment and its consequences, the restoration of attachment must be seen as the means of resolving the problem, since in this way missing growth may begin to be restored. It is nothing less than tragic that the attempted solution to a problem should be mistaken for the actual problem. The capacity for homosexual response is itself the reparative drive. The attempt to disrupt or suppress this response is in effect the attempt to ensure that the problem cannot be resolved.

A difficulty hitherto has stemmed from the fact that the overall phenomenon of same-sex ambivalence has so many different facets. This has inevitably led to one or more aspects being given undue prominence, in isolation from the phenomenon as a whole. Apparently contrary facts - in particular, love and hate towards the same love-source - have been found difficult to reconcile with each other in any meaningful way. Effects, e.g. the so-called 'mother-fixation' of the male homosexual, have been mistaken for causes. Explanations have dealt with intra-psychic transformations in isolation from genuinely interpersonal transactions. And, as we have just stated, the solution itself has been mistaken for the problem.

There is, moreover, a dichotomy between psychoanalysts and learning theorists in their understanding of the aetiology of homosexuality. Psychoanalytic authors would claim that early disturbances in parent-child relationships lead to subsequent homosexual orientation. Learning and social learning theorists would maintain that homosexuals have failed to learn appropriate behaviour for their sex. The learning process involves conditioning, and reinforcements of behaviour, leading to the establishment and confirmation of certain types of behaviour patterns. Moreover, the hypothesis of early trauma influencing subsequent patterns of behaviour is rejected, and thus a sharp contrast between the two approaches is postulated. Is this, however, justifiable? We wish to suggest here that it is not, and that on the present hypothesis the two approaches may well be correlated and co-ordinated.

A learning theorist would postulate that the development of gender identity and gender-appropriate behaviour is decisively influenced by observational learning and by processes of modelling. On this very hypothesis, however, is it not important to consider the possibility of the blocking or disruption of the learning process? A learning theorist is not, after all, committed to an understanding of positive learning alone. There is negative learning as well as positive learning, and it is precisely on the issue of negative learning that the concerns of analysts and of learning theorists should converge. Positive learning requires not merely the sheer presence of same-sex models, but also - most importantly - the ability to identify with them and thus to learn from them. Conversely, the learning process will be affected not merely by the absence of same-sex models, but - again, most significantly - by an inability to identify with such models even when they are available. This latter possibility has not yet been sufficiently taken into account, or indeed even isolated as a possible factor.

What we are postulating here is that traumatic disruption in relationship actually blocks the ability to identify, through repressing the capacity for attachment. Disidentification takes place, and hence the learning process is altered and radically diverted. Learning theorists have not yet done sufficient justice to the possibility of traumatic conditioning, i.e. negative learning. Trauma itself can thus be spoken of within the framework and terminology of learning theory. Disidentification due to unresolved trauma is itself a form of negative conditioning - a very severe and radical form of aversion conditioning, one might say.

It is important to remember that learning takes place in the context of, and through the medium of, personal relationships. It should be noted that the relationship may be satisfactory or in some degree unsatisfactory; in either case, the learning process can take place, though for better or for worse. But the case is different if the relationship has been fundamentally disrupted and not genuinely healed, despite, perhaps, some measure of subsequent adjustment on the surface. Even a bad relationship can allow for learning to take place. But a disrupted and non-existent relationship cannot, since here the defensive repression of the attachment need has radically affected the individual's actual capacity for relationship. The failure to learn what are considered appropriate behaviours stems from unresolved trauma, in that this has affected the very ability to learn.

Learning patterns are not to be considered in isolation from the relationships that form the actual matrix and channels of learning. It is the same-sex libidinal attachment that is itself identificatory. In the presence of such an attachment, external modelling may also be of value, secondarily. But in the absence of such an attachment, external modelling can at best be only superficial, since it is the attachment itself that is central and most crucial. Indeed, when disidentification has occurred, the presence of same-sex models may only confirm the disidentificatory impulse. This is because they are no longer understood as models for likeness, but on the contrary as models of what the person cannot be like, stemming from and reinforcing the aversive impulse. It would only be the restoration of attachment to such models that would be genuinely identificatory.

Disturbance in relationship leads to disturbance in learning patterns, and it is a weakness of behaviour therapy that it tries to modify the effects, but not their cause. This is further complicated by the common assumption that a defect in relating to the opposite sex is involved, rather than a defect in the same-sex relational capacity. For James (1967b) treatment implies:

> Firstly, the extinction of the homosexual response and, secondly, the extinction of avoidance responses to the opposite sex and the encouragement of approach responses. The extinction of the homosexual response is sometimes the sole method used.

Haynes (1970) assumes that the task is one of reducing or eliminating homosexual behaviour and promoting heterosexual behaviour. Mac Donough (1972) likewise speaks of avoidance conditioning and the need to promote the acquisition of approach responses to females. In each case the nature of the problem itself is radically misunderstood. The fundamental avoidance response in the homosexual is avoidance of the same sex, i.e. a defensive detachment resulting in same-sex ambivalence. It is this type of avoidance that requires to be overcome. Likewise, and in consequence of this, the requisite approach response to be promoted in the homosexual must be one of approach to the same sex. The love-response of the homosexual is itself the reparative attempt, and as such it is to be promoted and certainly not abrogated. The elimination of the homosexual response does not imply the elimination of the homosexual need, but merely its suppression. Thus, the person is confirmed in a state of incompletion by the suppression of the striving for completion. Moreover, to promote so-called heterosexual responses in such a person can never be more than relatively superficial, precisely because it is the attempt to elicit the responses of completion while forcing the person to remain in a state of incompletion. True heterosexuality, as distinct from pseudo-heterosexuality, presupposes the attainment of a heteropsychologic personality structure. And such a structure can only be attained by the fulfilment of same-sex, i.e. homosexual, personality needs.

For these reasons, we must consider the current typical aims of behaviour therapists vis-à-vis homosexuals as essentially counter-therapeutic. A misunderstanding of the nature of the problem leads to a misunderstanding of the nature of the solution. To abrogate the fulfilment of homosexual needs implies the confirmation of the individual in a *pre*-heterosexual position. To encourage such a person to make a closer acquaintance with the opposite sex can do nothing towards fulfilling same-sex deficits, and may even, especially in cases of radical disidentification, reinforce a sense of cross-gender identity. Increased contact with the opposite sex is by definition irrelevant to the problem of a disruption in a same-sex identificatory attachment.

James (1967b) states that homosexuality involves maladaptive responses that have been learned and can therefore be unlearned and replaced by newly learned responses. We would agree with this in principle, but not in detail. What in fact is it that has been learned and requires to be unlearned? The only maladaptive response that has been learned by the homosexual is a defensive detachment from the same sex, which has thwarted the fulfilment of homosexual needs and hence the attainment of heterosexuality. It is this traumatically based detachment, itself a form of aversion conditioning, that requires to be undone. A restored attachment to the same sex is to be promoted, of such a quality that missing growth is fully made up for, and thus heterosexuality may be attained.

We have emphasised the twofold nature of the problem in our discussion of same-sex ambivalence. The persisting defensiveness vis-à-vis the love-source is to be overcome and undone; in addition, the growth missed out through the disruption of attachment is to be made up for. It would be wrong to assume that the undoing of the defensive barrier would itself mark the resolution of the overall problem. It may facilitate resolution, but that is all. The person in question would still be in a state of incomplete growth until such time as this would be completed through the medium of a renewed attachment. The restoration of attachment does not instantly resolve the problem, since an attachment is a means (towards completion of growth) and not an end in itself. But the restoration of attachment begins to solve the problem, and without this the problem can never be solved.

Within the psychoanalytic frame of reference, the need to make up for missing growth is to be understood in terms of the development of the transference. In that the transference revives the residues of the past, it involves a potential for

working through both past distortion and past incompletion.
Distortion may be linked with the need to achieve insight, and
incompletion is to be correlated with the need to recapitulate
missing growth. In other words, there is a need both to undo
distortions of what has been, and to make up for and reconstruct
what has not yet been. The transference relationship, as a new
attachment, is itself the means for further growth. The use
of the transference is twofold, just as the nature of the problem
is twofold.

A renewed libidinal attachment is especially important in its
potential for meeting hitherto unmet dependency needs. Since
normal growth involves the fulfilment of dependency needs, the
disruption of normal growth involves a corresponding deficit in
this specific area. This may not always be very marked, but the
greater the degree of missing growth, the greater the remaining
dependency needs. In the area known as psychosis, this deficit
is particularly marked. Psychosis, in our view, involves a state
of radically incomplete growth. The pathological manifestations
of this may become apparent only in adult years, but the incompletion of growth has been present since early childhood, when
the process of growth was diverted from its normal course. The
meeting of dependency needs should be central to the treatment
of psychosis, and is significant to some degree in the treatment
of various disorders.

Unfortunately, the significance of this factor has not been
sufficiently recognised hitherto. Dependency needs may be
temporarily accepted, but are not encouraged. The rationale for
this lies in the desire to promote independence. We would agree
with this goal, but dispute the means used to promote this goal.
Independence grows from the fulfilment of dependency needs,
not from their abrogation. A dependent adult is someone in whom
dependency needs have not been fulfilled in the normal process
of growth.

It is important to consider the implications of this in the case
of radically incomplete growth. In a discussion of schizophrenia,
Limentani (1956) speaks of a feeling of fusion that may best be
described as 'symbiotic identification'. An overt psychosis
developed when some upset occurred in this relationship of the
patient with his mother. The patient would search for 'a strong
figure with whom to feel as one and with whom to establish a
new symbiotic identification'. This is considered to mark an
unconscious wish to remain a small child, rather than - as we
would view it - a realistic awareness of missing growth. As a
consequence, it seems entirely natural that such a person
should become 'dependent, borrowing strength by feeling that
he was part of the therapist', since on our account this would
mark the restoration of the normal process of growth. To accept
such needs only temporarily is to allow the process of growth to
begin, but not to continue. The patient's symbiotic relationship
is not 'a defense against the hostility resulting from early
deprivation', but simply the unmet dependency needs stemming

from early deprivation. Such deprivation may well also have
resulted in hostility, but missing growth is itself a consequence
of unresolved trauma, and not a defence against it.

Lidz (1975) speaks of the schizophrenic's egocentricity and
inability to differentiate between his mother's feelings and his
own.[1] Reality is distorted to his own needs and point of view[2]
- or, as we might say, the abiding psychological reality of
incomplete growth is insisted on. Lidz emphasises the importance
of forming boundaries between the self and others, and sees
the confusion of self and non-self as a matter of profound
regression. To speak of regression begs the question: a person
cannot strictly be said to regress to a point from which he may
never have advanced in the first place. More significantly, this
blurring or absence of ego-boundaries is not correlated, as it
should be, with abiding dependency needs. The 'absence of ego-
boundaries' marks a need for auxiliary ego-strength. It is not
per se abnormal, but rather the normal state of someone in whom
there are marked dependency needs, i.e. a young child or -
less usually - an adult whose psychological state is one of
radically incomplete growth. Auxiliary ego-strength is the
correlate of dependency needs, and it is provided by an attachment figure, when there is no defect in the capacity for relating
to such a figure. Lidz states:[3]

> Problems . . . arise because of the primitive character of the
> patient's attachment to his therapist. The patient's relatedness
> is more an anaclitic attachment than a transference relationship
> at the start. The patient may . . . be more interested in
> retaining the therapist than in engaging in psychotherapy.

This is neither illogical nor problematic, since the attachment
to the therapist is itself the fundamental form of therapy for
such persons. This is still a genuine transference, but one of a
more primitive nature than in persons where more growth may be
presupposed.

In her discussion of childhood psychosis Mahler (1969) notes:[4]

> The essential feature of symbiosis is . . . the delusion of a
> common boundary of the two actually and physically separate
> individuals.

And[5]

> An ego which is unable to function separately from the
> symbiotic partner tries to re-entrench itself in the delusional
> fantasy of oneness with the omnipotent mother, by coercing
> her into functioning as an extension of the self.

Again,[6]

> In the symbiotic psychotic syndrome, self-differentiation from

the mother during the separation-individuation phase has
failed, and the delusional symbiotic omnipotent fusion with the
mother is still being maintained.

We would not regard this as delusional, but as accurate to
intrapsychic reality. The growing ego is meant to develop 'in
tandem'. If the capacity for attachment is somehow affected,
the needs that are normally met through attachment must remain
unmet. The expression of an abiding need for a close and intense
attachment is quite realistic on this understanding. If separation-
individuation fails, it is because dependency needs are not any
longer being met. A person thus affected is dependent in the
sense of not being able to function independently, but that is all.
He is not dependent in the sense that his psychological dependency needs are in the process of being met. There is an unfortunate ambiguity in the term 'dependent', since it may in this way
be used to cover two entirely contrasting states. In the former
state, the solution must be one of restoring true dependency,
since true independence is the end-product of fulfilled dependency needs. The culmination of the process may not be achieved
if the process itself is abrogated short of fulfilment. The concept
of separation-individuation tends to be stated too absolutely. The
period of six to thirty months may mark a period of relative
individuation in the young child, but it is important to note that
the capacity for greater independence of behaviour is based on
a continuing state of close dependency. If absolute separation
takes place during this period, as in disidentification, the process of growing independence is terminated precisely because
its necessary substratum - of the continuing meeting of dependency needs - has been terminated.
  Moreover, it is important to pay attention to the father-child
relationship, as well as the mother-child relationship. A so-called
mother-fixation may not be pathological per se, but may mark a
defensive detachment from the father, as in the homosexual-
paranoid position in men and the heterosexual-paranoid position
in women. Socarides (1968b) and Stoller (1975) use Mahler's
concept of mother-child symbiosis for their discussion of male
homosexuality and transsexualism, without realising that in these
instances the mother-attachment is an effect of detachment from
the father. Alternatively, an apparent fixation to the mother may
mark an abiding need for attachment to her, a need based on
actual detachment from her. This would be true of the homosexual-paranoid position in women and the heterosexual-paranoid
position in men. These variations in detail should suggest
caution in the use of the term 'mother-fixation' as a generalisation.
  Why is early separation from mother or father traumatic? It is
because the growing ego of the young child requires auxiliary
ego-strength and is unable to function properly on its own. For
this reason other-loss is, of itself, ego-loss. The risk in separation is not just the immediate loss of auxiliary ego-strength,
but the possibility of permanently damaging the child's capacity

for attachment, i.e. of indefinitely prolonging the loss of auxiliary ego-strength, since the child is no longer able to relate (other than superficially) to the potential source of such strength.

The nature of the child's tie to his father as well as to his mother is to be seen in these terms. The psychological need for auxiliary ego-strength is as essential to the growing child as are physiological needs. Separation anxiety stems from the threat to auxiliary ego-strength. The pathological response to separation focuses on the child's attachment-need and attachment-capacity. The provision of auxiliary ego-strength is the central parental function; and the restoration of this should be a central therapeutic function, in order to make up for earlier deficits. Much of the therapeutic process should have the character of fostering or re-parenting.

A transference may arise in current relationships, based on incompletion in past relationships and marking a striving for completion. It is this striving for completion that we would see as the force underlying the creation of the transference, rather than a repetition compulsion as such (Freud, 1914a). The past is reactivated or 'repeated' only so long as it remains distorted or incomplete. The purpose of 'repetition' is to find the fulfilment not previously attained.

Transference arises spontaneously in all human relationships (Freud, 1910 [1909]). The therapeutic context may hope to provide a controlled transference, but it does not create the actual capacity for transference. Natural transferences are particularly noteworthy in the case of same-sex ambivalence. The reparative urge towards restoration of the same-sex attachment is a prime example of a positive transference being used to facilitate further growth. In other words, homosexual relationships are themselves natural transferences. They are positive so long as the reparative drive is predominant, but become negative transferences if the other side of the ambivalence emerges from repression. In either case, the current reality of relationship is shaped by the unmet needs, and distortions, of the past.

Taking this into the sphere of controlled transferences, it should become evident that there is a need for gender-specific therapy. A therapist of the same anatomic sex as the homosexual and transsexual is required, if deficits in same-sex attachment (and the needs met through same-sex attachment) are to be met. A therapist of the opposite anatomic sex cannot by definition cure homosexuality or transsexualism, as same-sex disidentification and ambivalence. The use of a therapist of the opposite sex might have been plausible when it was assumed that the disorder was one of relating to the opposite sex. Moreover, it is true that not all disorders require gender-specific therapy (though this might well be of greater value than previously realised). However, when the disorder is specifically a same-sex relational defect, together with the consequences of such a defect, it is only gender-specific therapy that can hope to achieve full healing. The very intensity of the natural gender-specific transferences that occur should encourage us to realise that here there is a therapeutic instrument of great potential.

It is clear that such natural transferences are rarely self-fulfilling. As already mentioned, they may be thwarted by the re-emergence of the negative side of the ambivalence; by the intensity of the dependency needs involved; and by the similarity of the needs of both partners in the relationship. This must not be taken to imply that a same-sex relationship is non-therapeutic, but rather that its great therapeutic value may be hindered by a variety of obstacles. A controlled gender-specific transference will still have to face the first two difficulties mentioned. However, unless the therapist is himself homosexual, the third difficulty will be obviated. A single-sex relationship in which one person is homosexual but the other is heterosexual, has thus a greater potential for stability than a single-sex relationship in which both partners are homosexual.

In parenthesis, this is not to assert that a homosexual thera-pist could not help a fellow-homosexual. Indeed, he would have the advantage of understanding the condition from within. The similarity of his own psychological needs might prove to be more of a limitation in some cases than in others. In any case, until heterosexual therapists are prepared to provide controlled single-sex relationships, the only kind of therapeutic relation-ship available to the homosexual will be the natural transference of an ordinary homosexual relationship, where, as it happens, emotional needs tend to be acted out sexually. A controlled gender-specific transference would seek to meet such needs without the overlay of secondary eroticisation.

A controlled single-sex relationship would permit of an intense attachment to be formed. The attachment as such is neither improper nor pathological, but simply the restoration of a normal attachment that was abnormally disrupted. Within the context of such an attachment, hitherto unmet needs for love, dependency and identity may begin to be met again.

The primary therapist in all cases of same-sex ambivalence should be a member of the same anatomic sex as the client. Granted this, there will also be scope for work by other thera-pists. Male and female co-therapists will be helpful through encouraging the underlying psychodynamics to become more evident: there is a flight from the same sex, which it is vital to interpret as such and not to mistake for a flight to the opposite sex. Opposite-sex therapists by themselves may provide general support or some more specific therapeutic help according to the individual's needs, but from the very nature of the problem must not usurp the central position of the same-sex therapist.

Where radical disidentification has taken place and marked dependency needs are involved, it will be necessary for the primary, same-sex therapist to undertake prolonged and intensive work with the client. A one-to-one relationship will be central, in that it aims to recapitulate the relation of parent and young child. Besides this central dyad, there may be some use of a triad, consisting of the primary dyad and one other same-sex therapist, i.e. this triad should involve co-therapists of the same sex, one of whom should be the primary therapist. This triad is to support and reinforce the work of the dyad, hence the inclusion of a therapist of the opposite sex would in this case be inappropriate, as diluting and indeed radically altering the requisite dynamics.

In the case of radical disidentification, a lengthy process of intensive therapy is likely to be indicated. A few years is probably the minimum requirement in such cases, and quite possibly longer. If this sounds excessive, it should be borne in mind that the normal process of growth for a young child takes the better part of the first two decades of life. Where unresolved trauma has blocked the normal process of growth since the age of two or three, it is quite unrealistic to expect this to be made up for in less than a few years. The process may be somewhat accelerated by the relative social maturity of the client, but it is bound to be lengthy. Length combined with intensity make this a difficult therapeutic proposition in view of available resources. But the task of reconstructing a human life can hardly be less than demanding, and would undoubtedly be an immensely rewarding enterprise.

In practice, there is of course a particular difficulty inherent in radical disidentification, which requires particular care in handling, viz. the defensive barrier. This may not present exceptional difficulties in lesser degrees of same-sex ambivalence, but in radical disidentification the defensive detachment is the condition known as paranoia, which has generally been labelled as incurable. However, this is but one side of the ambivalence. The defensive barrier implies an unmet love-need, and it should be possible to commence therapy by beginning to meet this unmet need and encouraging the development of a positive trans-ference. (This would also be true of heterosexual paranoia, which we are not discussing in detail here.) Indeed, even where paranoid symptoms are presented, their control must not be treated as an end in itself, but as a means towards facilitating the meeting of unmet attachment-needs.

Thus, the control of psychotic symptoms may be a necessary means towards healing, but is not to be confused with healing as such. Mere control of symptoms is not to be equated with the achievement of a post-psychotic state, but simply implies the restoration of a pre-psychotic state. A genuinely post-psychotic state would be psychologically rather than just temporally subsequent to psychosis, and would imply the actual resolution of the psychotic state. It will by no means be easy to achieve this goal, but its importance should by now be apparent, from our analysis of the meaning of the pre-psychotic state. This state implies a deeply repressed longing for love, a persisting defensiveness and negativity towards the love-source, and a radical absence of normal and necessary growth. Such a state is a human tragedy, whether or not accompanied by socially disturbing behaviour. The therapeutic goal cannot be merely social control, but must involve the resolution of the unmet love-need, with all that this implies. Nothing less than this may be regarded as true healing.

It will be evident that true healing is more readily to be achieved in the case of less radical disidentification, where neither the defensive barrier nor the corresponding deficit in growth are of marked severity. In principle, though, we would hope that any degree of disidentification could be healed, even if the therapeutic process may be long and complex in some cases.

7 SOME CONCLUSIONS

If healing is desirable, prevention is even more vital. The task
of undoing and making up for past deficits may often be obviated
right from the start, if more adequate care and precautions are
taken. Early separation of a child from a parent is particularly
significant. It is not being postulated that all such experiences
have serious pathological consequences, but that there is a
notable risk of pathological sequelae, and that it seems to be
largely a matter of luck as to whether or not the child overcomes
such a potentially traumatic event. The circumstances of such
trauma will also vary. A number of examples may be considered:

1 The illness of the child, especially when this involves
hospitalisation, i.e. a large measure of separation from parental
care.

2 The illness of a parent. Even when this does not involve
hospitalisation, it may mark a period of inability to care for the
young child, which may in turn affect the child's capacity for
attachment to the parent.

3 The birth of a sibling, especially when this involves the
mother's absence due to hospitalisation, or a conspicuous lessen-
ing in the amount of care she gives to the child she has already.

4 The temporary, prolonged, or permanent absence of a
parent.

5 The separation or divorce of the parents.

6 The death of a parent.

7 Adoption, fostering, or living in an orphanage.

8 Being brought up by a succession of nurses, governesses,
etc., i.e. a constantly changing succession of 'parental' figures.

9 Ill-treatment by a parent.

It should be noted that in the majority of these instances the
traumatic event is or may be involuntary. Deliberate ill-treatment is but one possible cause of a rupture in attachment. (For
this reason it may be considered that the Schreber case is in
fact atypical as an example of radical disidentification. Actual
separation would more usually cause this condition.) The
question of the parent's responsibility will arise in some instances
- perhaps more frequently as regards lesser degrees of disidentification - but in some cases no responsibility can be
allocated. A human tragedy does not always stem from human
culpability.

In some instances some responsibility may be allocated
indirectly, as where a marriage fails and the child suffers as a
result of this. It is true that not every marriage that stays to-

gether provides a suitable environment for children, but in
theory the availability of two parents is the ideal for human
growth, since in this way each child has an attachment-figure
of the same sex and of the opposite sex to relate to (provided
that the actual capacity for attachment is not damaged).

The effects of temporary separation may to some extent be
mitigated by substitute care, from relatives or other persons.
Despite this, some risk of trauma will remain, since it is not just
care as such, but the source of care, that is significant. In
this way, substitute care cannot fully make up for a specific
attachment. The risk in separation is not that the child may be
neglected, but that the specific attachment may not be maintained and reinforced; and that the absence of the specific
attachment-figure may result in long-term damage to the child's
capacity for attachment. There is no determinism in this. Sometimes there may be little damage or the trauma may be resolved
spontaneously. But there is a risk of serious damage, which
requires that far more attention should be paid to events with
a high pathogenic potential. Frequent visits when a child or
parent is hospitalised should be not merely encouraged, but
actively promoted (and, if necessary, subsidised), as being
vital to the maintenance of psychological well-being. And, when
possible, separations should be minimised or avoided. It is
temporary separations, and not just prolonged ones, that are
highly pathogenic for the young child, and it has been a mistake
hitherto to underestimate their significance, as Mahler, for
instance, does:[1]

> The anamneses of children with predominantly autistic or
> primarily symbiotic psychosis did not indicate, or only very
> rarely, that separation of any significant duration from the
> mother had actually occurred. In the majority of these cases,
> there was no real loss of the symbiotic object. I refer to such
> ubiquitous traumata as transient separation from the mother
> due to the birth of a sibling or due to hospitalization of
> either mother or child . . . Since real and prolonged separation
> from the mother was conspicuously absent in the anamneses
> of our psychotic children, it must be emphasized that actual
> object loss was not an aetiological factor in their psychotic
> break with reality.

Such a statement rests on an inability to recognise that any
separation may be 'significant' and 'real' for the young child. A
temporary separation does not always or necessarily result in
pathological consequences, but it would be equally mistaken to
assume, as Mahler does here, that such a separation *cannot* have
such consequences. The risk is there, even if - fortunately -
it does not always materialise.

The pathological effects of childhood trauma may only become
apparent in later years, but the actual damage to the personality
has been there since early childhood, even if masked by a super-

ficial adjustment. However, if therapy is undertaken in early
years, this makes a difference of some significance to the therapeutic goal. In all cases, whether children or adults, unresolved
trauma requires to be resolved. But the earlier therapy is
undertaken, the less is the extent of missing growth. If the
process of normal growth was in some significant respect blocked
at age two, the adult thus affected requires to make up for all
the growth that was missed during childhood and adolescence.
However the child thus affected may only require to make up
for a few years of missing growth, after which the process of
growth may be resumed in the normal way.

It is generally considered that the fundamental sense of gender
identity - core gender identity - is firmly established in the
early years of life:

> Though gender imprinting begins by the first birthday, the
> critical period is reached by about the age of eighteen months.
> By the age of two and one-half years, gender role is already
> well established. (Money, Hampson and Hampson, 1955b).

We would agree with this as a general proposition, but its
implications require careful scrutiny. Subsequent to the
establishment of core gender identity, a change of gender role
that is imposed by the decision of others is probably not feasible.
The fundamental sense of gender identity may not, once
established, be arbitrarily reversed. However, one may not
assume that it is altogether irreversible. Gender role may be well
established by the age of two-and-a-half, but it is not, however,
safely established. The future transsexual has as normal an
identity as anyone else until disidentification takes place. As a
general statement we may say that gender identity is irreversible
except by trauma that disrupts the identificatory attachment to
the parent of the same sex.
    The early years are particularly vulnerable to such trauma,
since a defensive detachment at this age disrupts the identificatory process only shortly after it has commenced. Moreover,
this does not imply a genuine reversal of identity. The transsexual does not acquire a true cross-gender identity, but is
merely aware of a radical absence of same-sex identity. The
longing for an identificatory attachment to a member of the same
anatomic sex may be repressed, but the transsexual is still
essentially a member of his own anatomic sex, even if a thwarted
and radically incomplete member. Despite appearances, the
transsexual is no real exception to the general rule that gender
identity tends to be congruent with physiological sexuality.
The fact that this tendency may be repressed and not attain
fulfilment does not deny this general rule, but rather provides
a paradoxical confirmation of it.
    What is philosophically more puzzling than transsexualism is
the occurrence of discrepant identities in members of the physio-

logical intersexes (hermaphrodites). Where the gender identity
accords with both the role of assignment and rearing and also
with the preponderance of physiological sexuality, this problem
does not arise. However, it is clear that as a general rule
hermaphrodites develop a sense of identity in accordance with
the role of assignment and rearing, even when this disagrees
with significant physiological variables (Money, Hampson and
Hampson, 1957). Why this should happen is something that we
are unable to answer here. The fact that a minority of hermaphrodites develop an identity different from their assigned role
but congruent with certain physiological characteristics, seems
less problematical. One may hypothesise here that, despite the
assigned role, a different identity is in fact being received
through the process of attachment, even if this only becomes
apparent in later years. Such examples might be seen as con-
sistent with the general rule of identity congruent with physiological sexuality.

This does not, of course, account for hermaphrodite identities
that are established contrary to certain significant aspects of
physiological sexuality. But the occurrence of these may not in
any case be taken to imply that the role of assignment and rearing is more significant generally than physiological criteria of
sexuality. It is difficult to see how far one may legitimately
extrapolate from the physiological intersexes. The fact remains
that for the vast majority of the human race gender identity
tends to be congruent with physiological sexuality. Transsexualism has been shown to be no true exception to this; and
large numbers of hermaphrodites (those correctly assigned;
and those who develop an identity congruent with preponderant
physiology despite their assignment) are likewise no exception
to this general rule. If the role of assignment and rearing were
crucial, this would imply that any physiologically normal child
could be brought up as a member of the opposite sex and
develop an identity as such. Obviously, such an experiment
would never be undertaken, for ethical reasons. But one might
venture to predict that in any case the experiment would fail.
The evidence to date is insufficient to suggest that gender
identity is capable of random assignment, or that there is no
innate or instinctual basis for it. The evidence provided by
transsexualism and homosexuality is that mature gender identity
requires a lengthy process of gender identification, which may
in some cases be disrupted. But the direction for development,
whether this is fulfilled or repressed, is a given fact and has
not been a matter of choice.

Identity is received through the medium of an attachment.
This still leaves unanswered the question of why a boy receives
masculinity through his attachment to his father, while a girl
does not receive masculinity through her attachment to her
father. This is obviously a matter for further research, but here
we will suggest that there would seem to be some predisposition
involved, which learning alone may not account for. A masculine

physiology generally predisposes a person to receive masculinity through a masculine attachment (but not femininity through a feminine attachment). A feminine physiology generally predisposes a person to receive femininity through a feminine attachment (but not masculinity through a masculine attachment). This general predisposition may tentatively be termed a bio-psychic tendency.

There is a vital difference between an identity that has been received through an attachment, and an apparent identity (more truly, an absence of identity) that is based on a defensive detachment. In the latter case, there remains (though it is sometimes repressed) a reparative striving for identification, stemming from the state of incompletion. A mature identity is non-reparative. It might be of value to investigate whether hermaphrodite identities, especially discrepant identities, are actually non-reparative. They may in fact be so, or some may prove not to be so, but the point is that this particular question has not as yet been asked or answered. If a non-reparative identity has been established, this provides a strong argument for allowing the person to live in a role that accords with this identity, if they are not already doing so. Gender reassignment in such an instance would confirm a complete identity, rather than – as in the case of transsexuals – a radically incomplete one.

At present, gender reassignment surgery for transsexuals marks the culmination of the disidentificatory impulse. Surgical measures have been adopted on a pragmatic basis as the best available method of treatment, since the overwhelming consensus of expert opinion has been that transsexualism is inaccessible to psychotherapy or to any other known method of therapy. In our present study, we have indicated that an alternative is available, at least in theory, for the transsexual. An identity congruent with physiological sexuality may be reconstructed through a long and complex process of therapy, of a more intensive nature than much therapy as currently practised. This will in fact meet, rather than thwart, the transsexual's own deepest longings (for a same-sex attachment and hence for identificatory growth). At the same time, there is a risk that the therapist may not be able to deal with the negative side of the transference, so this form of therapy is not to be lightly embarked upon.

Surgery for hermaphrodites is not an entirely comparable matter. If, in some instances, disidentification has taken place, the person will be essentially transsexual or homosexual as well as hermaphrodite. Where disidentification is not involved, a non-reparative identity should be confirmed, on the assumption that when the identificatory process has been genuinely completed, it cannot be undone. Corrective surgery for hermaphrodite children may be undertaken to confirm or to correct the gender of assignment, but here another consideration arises. It is often suggested that it is desirable for such surgery to be undertaken as early as possible (Money, Hampson and Hampson, 1955a, 1957; Jones and Verkauf, 1970). The assumption is that early surgery will minimise the risk of undesirable psychological consequences from physiological ambiguities. This may be the case, but we have already indicated that early hospitalisation for whatever reason is itself potentially pathogenic. A child with physiological ambiguities but also a continuing attachment to his parents will be psychologically more healthy than a child in whom such ambiguities have been corrected, but at the cost of disrupting a parental attachment.

Although this risk may not always materialise, it is not to be minimised. An example of this kind of development is reported by Lewis et al. (1970). A female with the adrenogenital syndrome was declared male at birth and reassigned female at five months. Corrective surgery took place at age three-and-a-half. Many months of her first years were spent in hospital, harnessed to a metabolism bed for urine collection. Her later history showed a serious inability to accept her femininity, with suicidal tendencies and severe agoraphobia. On such evidence as is available, this case report suggests precisely the kind of pathological development we have warned against. In view of this risk, we would not recommend early surgery for hermaphroditic children. Hospitalisation during the first five or six years of life is to be avoided if at all possible.

Sexuality in the adult is intended to be the expression of a fulfilled, i.e. non-reparative, identity. Where the normal process of growth has taken place unhindered, the process of same-sex identification will have been completed; and hence the same-sex attachment - through which such an identity is attained - will have become redundant, through the fulfilment of its purpose. The process of identification should take place through an uninterrupted parent-child attachment, and in the majority of cases this does in fact take place. However, in a number of instances it is clear that the process of identification-through-attachment has not been completed by the time that adult years are reached. Psychological needs that are essentially non-adult remain in a person who is in other respects adult. But to attempt to meet these psychological needs through the medium of sexual expression is to mistake the character of these needs. It is understandable that someone who has attained physiological maturity should interpret libidinal needs as sexual. However, this secondary eroticisation of outstanding deficits in growth is essentially a confusion: the emotional needs of the non-adult are confused with the physiological desires of the adult. This is not to deny the importance of a close emotional bond as a means of overcoming past deficits. But these legitimate libidinal needs could well be met without eroticisation.

Sexual expression is not appropriate to the normal parent-child relationship and, as a corollary to this, sexual expression is not appropriate to any relationship which attempts to meet non-adult attachment needs. A relationship for the attainment of identity is not to be confused with a relationship which expresses an identity already attained. Is any given relationship based on an incomplete identity and therefore reparative, or on a complete identity and therefore non-reparative? A reparative relationship is not to be eroticised. Rather, needs for reparative growth should be fulfilled (non-sexually) and thus the basis for a sexually-expressed relationship will be attained. Sexuality is meant to be non-reparative, i.e. it should express the desires both of physiological maturity and also of psychological maturity. The two should be co-ordinated, rather than the former isolated from the latter. In the absence of such co-ordination, sexual expression must necessarily be of a relatively superficial nature, since its psychological basis is incomplete.

Homosexual relationships are inherently self-limiting. First, the re-emergence of the negative side of the ambivalence may disrupt the attachment short of its fulfilment. Second, if a negative transference is somehow negotiated and attachment-needs are fulfilled, the attachment will have made itself redundant. The fulfilment of homosexuality is itself the attainment of heterosexuality – not a premature attempt to make persons who are still homosexual behave heterosexually, but the fulfil-ment of homo-emotional needs and hence the attainment of a genuinely heteropsychologic personality structure. Heterosexual relationships may be stable or unstable, according to the qualities of the individuals concerned, but they are not in-herently self-limiting as homosexual relationships are of their very nature.

Sexual orientation is an expression of gender identity. Where this identity is incomplete, there is a reparative striving towards the fulfilment of the identificatory process. Instinctual drives are to be linked with their interpersonal fulfilment, or lack of fulfilment. Identity is attained through a libidinal attachment to a member of one's own sex. Object-choice is a function of one's own identity: homosexual object-choice stems from an incomplete identity, and truly heterosexual object-choice is based on the completion of the gender identificatory process. Rosen (1974) states that 'the only difference between the lesbian and other women is the choice of love object.'[2] This is precisely the point at issue, since underlying this difference of object-choice there is a fundamental difference of personality structure between the homosexual and the heterosexual.

Some persons may be categorised as bisexual. Where this is not merely superficial, it may be taken to mark a partial fulfilment of homo-emotional needs sufficient to promote heterosexual activity. However, to the extent that homo-emotional needs have not been fulfilled, there is a corresponding absence of a heteropsychologic personality structure, and hence true hetero-sexuality has not yet been attained. Bisexuality may not be understood as involving both true heterosexuality and true

homosexuality - on an equal basis, as it were - since this would
be a contradiction in terms. Continuing homosexuality implies
that a heteropsychologic structure has not yet been attained.
Heterosexuality would imply that homo-emotional needs have in
fact been fulfilled. The bisexual is not yet truly heterosexual,
but the underlying state of incompletion may be less than in
most homosexuals.

It is often suggested that we are all bisexual. This idea of a
universal bisexuality is an imprecise concept, and for this
reason not particularly helpful. Its physiological application
derives from the discovery that the urogenital systems of the
two sexes derive from a common embryonic origin. However, as
Rado (1940) notes:

> In the final shaping of the normal individual, the double
> embryological origin of the genital system does not result in
> any physiological duality of reproductive functioning.

As a psychological concept, bisexuality may be given various
interpretations, but is most commonly taken to imply that the
adult has a potential for sexual expression vis-à-vis members of
both sexes. In view of the present study, such a statement
must be regarded as untrue. The attainment of heterosexuality
implies the fulfilment of homo-emotional needs, so that a same-sex
attachment is no longer required in order to fulfil those needs.
The adult whose homo-emotional needs have been fulfilled no
longer has a potential for sexual expression towards members of
his own sex. Bisexuality is neither universal nor normative,
but marks the incompletion of the normal process of psychological
growth. Ford and Beach (1965) state:[3]

> Men and women who are totally lacking in any conscious homo-
> sexual leanings are as much a product of cultural conditioning
> as are the exclusive homosexuals who find heterosexual
> relations distasteful and unsatisfying. Both extremes represent
> movement away from the original, intermediate condition which
> includes the capacity for both forms of sexual expression.

It is not cultural conditioning, but the vicissitudes of psychological development, that account for exclusive heterosexuality
and exclusive homosexuality. In the former instance, the process
of identificatory growth has been completed; in the latter, it is
still decisively incomplete. The assumption that there is an
'original, intermediate condition' must be regarded as unfounded.
No one who has attained true heterosexuality can be bisexual
or latently homosexual.

In connection with this, it should be added that numbers alone
do nothing to prove the normality of homosexuality. Although
the incidence of homosexuality is undoubtedly considerable
(Kinsey et al. 1953a, 1953b), it is a logical fallacy to assume that
sheer numbers imply a normative character. If a substantial

minority of the population developed a particular disease, this would not imply the normality of such a disease. This is not to suggest that homosexuality is a disease, but is to indicate that arguments of normality based on frequency of incidence merely beg the question.

The occurrence of homosexuality does imply pathology, but it is crucial to distinguish between what is and what is not pathological in the homosexual condition. What is pathological is the defensive detachment from the love-source, and the missing growth consequent on this. Needs for love, dependency and identification which are normally met through the medium of an attachment to a (parental) love-source of the same sex, have remained unmet. The capacity for same-sex love is the attempt to restore this disrupted attachment and hence to make up for missing growth. Thus, the homosexual response is not itself the problem, but rather the attempted solution to the problem. It is itself the reparative drive towards restoration; it presupposes an underlying pathology, but is not itself pathological. It is vital to take this into account.

Psychological testing does not necessarily provide evidence of pathology in homosexuals. This may in part be due to the limitations of the tests themselves, but another reason may be the non-pathological nature of the homosexual love-response. If the person tested is someone currently involved in a positive homosexual relationship, the therapeutic effect of this natural transference may be sufficient to mask the underlying pathology. (By way of analogy, tests for physical disorder will produce different results according to whether the individual is currently receiving medication or not.)

Rosen (1974) regards lesbianism as a way of life, rather than as a sickness.[4] We would not regard homosexuality as merely an alternative life-style, but to speak of it as a sickness may be equally misleading. The overall homosexual phenomenon, of same-sex ambivalence, involves both a problem and its cure. The homosexual love-response in itself is the means of healing, and not the problem.

In conclusion, we must reiterate that homosexuality and a fortiori transsexualism involve a defect in the relational capacity vis-à-vis the same sex. Freud (1905) states:[5]

> No doubt the strongest force working against a permanent inversion of the sexual object is the attraction which the opposing sexual characters exercise upon one another.

Unless it is merely tautologous, asserting that heterosexual object choice is promoted by the growth of heterosexuality, this statement is mistaken. Most particularly, it begs the question. For members of the sexes to be truly 'other' and 'opposite', a same-sex identity must first have been attained. When the same-sex identificatory process is still in some degree incomplete, one is unable to relate to the opposite sex as a psychologically complete member of one's own sex. Conversely, however, if homosexual needs are really fulfilled, heterosexuality will take care of itself, since heterosexuality is the relational capacity of someone in whom homosexual needs have been fulfilled. A heteropsychologic personality structure cannot be achieved by the abrogation of homosexual needs, but through their fulfilment, and only through their fulfilment.

Normal and universal needs are involved in homosexuality. What is abnormal is that these needs should have been left unmet and not fulfilled in the normal way and at the normal time, i.e. in childhood and adolescence, through the attachment to the parent of the same sex. The adult heterosexual is someone who has had these needs and in whom they have been fulfilled. In this particular sense, every adult who is not homosexual may be termed ex-homosexual, i.e. someone whose needs for an identificatory attachment have been met and fulfilled. The adult homosexual is someone in whom these needs have not (yet) been met. It is not the needs as such that are pathological, but their lack of fulfilment.

An analogy that we may use in the evaluation of homosexuality (and transsexualism) is that of the orphan. Although this condition is unfortunate, it is not a matter of the orphan's personal culpability. One would not think of punishing the orphan for being an orphan. Likewise with the homosexual. The analogy in fact proves to be particularly close, since the homosexual has suffered from some deficit in the parent-child relationship (whether or not this was wilful on the part of the parent). The homosexual may thus be understood as a kind of psychological orphan. In the case of radical disidentification, this state of orphanhood is particularly severe. The question to be asked here (and to a lesser degree in lesser states of disidentification) is this: Should a boy of two or three be permanently deprived of his father? Should a girl of two or three be permanently deprived of her mother? If your answer to this is no, you may not condemn the homosexual response, since this is itself the solution to precisely this kind of problem.

NOTES

CHAPTER 1   THE SCHREBER CASE
1   Freud, 1911, p. 79.
2   Freud, 1937a, p. 267.
3   Freud, 1937a, p. 268.
4   Schatzman, 1973, pp. 130-1.
5   Ibid., p. 131.
6   Freud, 1911, p. 63.
7   Ibid., p. 63.
8   Bowlby, 1973, p. 249.

CHAPTER 2   THE STRUCTURES OF AMBIVALENCE
1   Schmideberg (1931) and Bollmeier (1938) discuss cases of paranoia with
    overt homosexuality.

CHAPTER 3   DISIDENTIFICATION
1   Stoller, 1975, p. 239.
2   Green and Money (eds), 1969, p. 286.
3   See Green and Money (eds), (1969), Ch. 4.

CHAPTER 4   THE MALE HOMOSEXUAL
1   Fenichel, 1945a, p. 334.
2   Bieber et al., 1962, p. 157.
3   Ibid., p. 253.
4   Bergler, 1961, p. 204.
5   Ibid.
6   Fenichel, 1945a, p. 335.
7   Ibid., p. 337.
8   Bieber et al., 1962, p. 44.
9   Ibid., p. 104.
10 Ibid., p. 115.
11 Ibid., p. 179, p. 311.
12 Ibid., p. 172.
13 Ibid., pp. 303-4.
14 Fenichel, 1945a, p. 334.
15 Bieber et al., 1962, pp. 231, 235, 314.
16 Bieber et al., 1962.

CHAPTER 5   THE FEMALE HOMOSEXUAL
1   West, 1977, p. 191.
2   Bergler, 1961, p. 338.
3   Ibid., p. 343.
4   Ibid., p. 342.
5   Ibid., pp. 354-5.
6   Ibid., p. 361.
7   Socarides, 1968a, p. 21.
8   Ibid., p. 197.
9   Ibid., p. 87.
10 Ibid., p. 176.
11 Ibid., p. 198.
12 Ibid., p. 175.
13 Ibid., p. 88.
14 Ibid., p. 174.

15 Ibid., p. 176.
16 Henry, 1950, p. 936.
17 Fenichel, 1945a, p. 345.
18 West, 1977, p. 90.
19 See Green and Money (eds), 1969, p. 86.
20 Storr, 1964, p. 76.
21 Bowlby, 1973, p. 246.
22 Storr, 1964, p. 76.
23 Walinder, 1967, p. 50.
24 Socarides, 1968a, p. 172.
25 Barnhouse, 1977, p. 88.
26 Ibid., p. 88.
27 Barnhouse, 1977, p. 77.
28 Ibid., p. 78.
29 Ibid., p. 79.
30 Lorand and Balint (eds), (1965), pp. 131-59.
31 Ibid., p. 144.
32 Barnhouse, 1977, p. 91.
33 Ibid., p. 174.

CHAPTER 6   TOWARDS THE HEALING OF THE DEEPLY WOUNDED
1 Lidz 1975, p. 11.
2 Ibid., p. 55.
3 Ibid., p. 107.
4 Mahler, 1969, p. 9.
5 Ibid., p. 42.
6 Ibid., p. 74.

CHAPTER 7   SOME CONCLUSIONS
1 Mahler, 1969, p. 51.
2 Rosen 1974, p. 65.
3 Ford and Beach, 1965, p. 277.
4 Rosen, 1974, p. 65.
5 Freud, 1905, p. 229.

BIBLIOGRAPHY

Acosta, Frank X. (1975), Etiology and treatment of homosexuality: a review, 'Archives of Sexual Behavior', 4, 9-29.

Ainsworth, M.D. Salter (1969), Object relations, dependency, and attachment: a theoretical review of the infant-mother relationship, 'Child Development', 40, 969-1025.

Akesson, H.O. and Walinder, J. (1969), Transsexualism. Effect on rate and density-pattern of change of residence, 'British Journal of Psychiatry', 115, 593-4.

Alanen, Yrjo O. (1956), On the personality of the mother and early mother-child relationship of 100 schizophrenic patients, 'Acta Psychiatrica et Neurologica Scandinavica, Supplementum', 106, 227-34.

Alger, Ian (1960), Therapy with schizophrenic patients, 'American Journal of Orthopsychiatry', 30, 521-27.

Allen, Clifford (1952), The problems of homosexuality, 'International Journal of Sexology', 6, 40-2.

— (1958), 'Homosexuality: its nature, causation and treatment', London, Staples Press.

— (1969), 'A textbook of psychosexual disorders', London, Oxford University Press.

Alpert, Augusta (1959), Reversibility of pathological fixations associated with maternal deprivation in infancy, 'Psychoanalytic Study of the Child', 14, 169-85.

Anchersen, Per (1956), Problems of transvestism, 'Acta Psychiatrica et Neurologica Scandinavica, Supplementum', 106, 249-56.

Anderson, Charles (1949), Aspects of pathological grief and mourning, 'International Journal of Psycho-analysis', 30, 48-55.

Angelino, Henry and Shedd, Charles L. (1955), A note on Berdache, 'American Anthropologist', 57, 121-5.

Archibald, Herbert C., Bell, Dorothy, Miller, Christine and Tuddenham, Read D. (1962), Bereavement in childhood and adult psychiatric disturbance, 'Psychosomatic Medicine', 24, 343-51.

Armstrong, C.N. (1966), Treatment of wrongly assigned sex, 'British Medical Journal', 2, 1255-6.

Ashworth, A.E. and Walker, W.M. (1972), Social structure and homosexuality: a theoretical appraisal, 'British Journal of Sociology', 23, 146-58.

Azima, H. and Wittkower, E.D. (1956), Gratification of basic needs in treatment of schizophrenics, 'Psychiatry', 19, 121-9.

Bacon, Catherine (1965), A developmental theory of female homosexuality, in Lorand and Balint (eds), 'Perversions: psychodynamics and therapy'.

Bak, Robert (1939), Regression of ego-orientation and libido in schizophrenia, 'International Journal of Psycho-analysis', 20, 64-71.

— (1946), Masochism in paranoia, 'Psychoanalytic Quarterly', 15, 285-301.

Baker, Howard J. (1969), Transsexualism - problems in treatment, 'American Journal of Psychiatry', 125, 1412-18.

Bakwin, Harry (1968), Deviant gender-role behavior in children: relation to homosexuality, 'Pediatrics', 41, 620-9.

Balint, Alice (1949), Love for the mother and mother love, 'International Journal of Psycho-analysis', 30, 251-9.

Balint, Michael (1949), Early developmental states of the ego. Primary object love, 'International Journal of Psycho-analysis', 30, 265-73.

Bancroft, John (1969), Aversion therapy of homosexuality, 'British Journal of Psychiatry', 115, 1417-31.

— (1970), Homosexuality in the male, 'British Journal of Hospital Medicine',
3, 168-81.
— (1978), Gender identity and sexual dysfunction in the male, in 'Society,
Stress and Disease', Vol. 3 'The productive and reproductive age - male/
female roles and relationships', ed. Lennart Levi, London, Oxford University
Press.
Barahal, Hyman S. (1953), Female transvestism and homosexuality, 'Psychiatric
Quarterly', 27, 390-438.
Barker, J.C. (1966), Transsexualism and transvestism, 'Journal of the
American Medical Association', 198, 488.
Barlow, David H., Reynolds, E. Joyce and Agras, W. Stewart (1973), Gender
identity change in a transsexual, 'Archives of General Psychiatry', 28, 569-76.
Barnes, Mary and Berke, Joseph (1974), 'Mary Barnes', Harmondsworth,
Penguin.
Barnhouse, Ruth Tiffany (1977), 'Homosexuality: a symbolic confusion', New
York, Seabury Press (Crossroad Books).
Barno, Alex (1962), Testicular feminization syndrome in male pseudohermaphro-
dites, 'American Journal of Obstetrics and Gynaecology', 84, 710-18.
Bateson, Gregory, Jackson, Don D., Haley, Jay and Weakland, John (1956),
Toward a theory of schizophrenia, 'Behavioral Science', 1, 251-64.
Baumeyer, Franz (1956), The Schreber case, 'International Journal of Psycho-
analysis', 37, 61-74.
Beckett, Peter G.S., Robinson, David B., Frazier, Shervert H., Steinhilber,
Richard M., Duncan, Glen M., Estes, Hubert R., Litin, Edward M., Grattan,
Robert T., Lorton, William L., Williams, George E. and Johnson, Adelaide
M. (1956), The significance of exogenous traumata in the genesis of
schizophrenia, 'Psychiatry', 19, 137-42.
Beilin, Leon M. and Grueneberg, Julius (1948), Genital self-mutilation by
mental patients, 'Journal of Urology', 59, 635-41.
Bell, Alan P. (1972), Human sexuality - a response, 'International Journal of
Psychiatry', 10, 99-102.
— (1975), Research in homosexuality: back to the drawing board, 'Archives
of Sexual Behavior', 4, 421-31.
Bell, Alan P. and Weinberg, Martin S. (1978) 'Homosexualities', London,
Mitchell Beazley.
Bender, Lauretta (1970), The life course of schizophrenic children, 'Biological
Psychiatry', 2, 165-172.
— (1971), Alpha and omega of childhood schizophrenia, 'Journal of Autism and
Childhood Schizophrenia', 1, 115-18.
Bender, Lauretta and Yarnell, Helen (1941), An observation nursery, 'American
Journal of Psychiatry', 97, 1158-74.
Bene, Eva (1965a), On the genesis of male homosexuality: an attempt at
clarifying the role of the parents, 'British Journal of Psychiatry', 111,
803-13.
— (1965b), On the genesis of female homosexuality, 'British Journal of
Psychiatry', 111, 815-21.
Benjamin, Harry (1966), 'The transsexual phenomenon', New York, Julian
Press.
— (1967), Transvestism and transsexualism in the male and female, 'Journal
of Sex Research', 3, 107-27.
— (1969), Newer aspects of the transsexual phenomenon, 'Journal of Sex
Research', 5, 135-44.
Bentinck, Richard C., Lisser, H. and Reilly, William A. (1956), Female
pseudo-hermaphrodism with penile urethra, masquerading as precocious
puberty and cryptorchidism, 'Journal of Clinical Endocrinology and
Metabolism', 16, 412-18.
Beres, David and Obers, Samuel J. (1950), The effects of extreme deprivation
in infancy on psychic structure in adolescence, 'Psychoanalytic Study of
the Child', 5, 212-35.
Berg, Ian, Nixon, Harold H. and MacMahon, Robert (1963), Change of assigned
sex at puberty, 'Lancet', 2, 1216-17.

Bergler, Edmund (1954), Spurious homosexuality, 'Psychiatric Quarterly, Supplement', 28, 68-77.
— (1961), 'Counterfeit-Sex', New York, Grove Press and London, Evergreen Books.
Berke, Joseph H. (1977), 'Butterfly Man', London, Hutchinson.
Bieber, Irving et al. (1962), 'Homosexuality: a psychoanalytic study', New York, Basic Books.
— (1972), Homosexual dynamics in psychiatric crisis, 'American Journal of Psychiatry', 128, 1268-72.
Biller, Henry B. (1970), Father absence and the personality development of the male child, 'Developmental Psychology', 2, 181-201.
Birk, Lee, Miller, Elizabeth and Cohler, Bertram (1970), Group psychotherapy for homosexual men by male-female cotherapists, 'Acta Psychiatrica Scandinavica, Supplementum', 218, 1-38.
Bisset, R.D.N. (1949), Self-castration, 'British Medical Journal', 2, 59.
Blacker, K.H. and Wong, N. (1963), Four cases of autocastration, 'Archives of General Psychiatry', 8, 169-76.
Bleuler, Manfred (1931), Schizophrenia, 'Archives of Neurology and Psychiatry', . 26, 610-27.
Boehm, Felix (1930), The femininity complex in men, 'International Journal of Psycho-analysis', 11, 444-69.
Bogdan, Robert (ed.) (1974), 'Being different', New York, Wiley-Interscience.
Bollmeier, L.N. (1938), A paranoid mechanism in male overt homosexuality, 'Psychoanalytic Quarterly', 7, 357-67.
Bosselman, Beulah Chamberlain (1960), Castration anxiety and phallus envy: a reformulation, 'Psychiatric Quarterly', 14, 252-59.
Botwinick, J. and Machover, S. (1951), A psychometric examination of latent homosexuality in alcoholism, 'Quarterly Journal of Studies on Alcohol', 12, 268-72.
Bowlby, John (1940), The influence of early environment in the development of neurosis and neurotic character, 'International Journal of Psycho-analysis', 21, 154-78.
— (1953), Some pathological processes set in train by early mother-child separation, 'Journal of Mental Science', 99, 265-72.
— (1957), An ethological approach to research in child development, 'British Journal of Medical Psychology', 30, 230-40.
— (1958), The nature of the child's tie to his mother, 'International Journal of Psycho-analysis', 39, 350-73.
— (1960), Grief and mourning in infancy and early childhood, 'Psychoanalytic Study of the Child', 15, 9-52.
— (1961), Separation anxiety: a clinical review of the literature, 'Journal of Child Psychology and Psychiatry', 1, 251-69.
— (1963), Pathological mourning and childhood mourning, 'Journal of the American Psychoanalytic Association', 11, 500-41.
— (1973), 'Separation, anxiety and anger', London, Hogarth Press.
Bowlby, John, Ainsworth, Mary, Boston, Mary and Rosenbluth, Dina (1956), The effects of mother-child separation: a follow-up study, 'British Journal of Medical Psychology', 29, 211-47.
Bowlby, John, Robertson, James and Rosenbluth, Dina (1952), A two-year-old goes to hospital, 'Psychoanalytic Study of the Child', 7, 82-94.
Bowman, Karl M. and Engle, Bernice (1957), Medicolegal aspects of transvestism, 'American Journal of Psychiatry', 113, 583-8.
— (1960), Sex offenses: the medical and legal implications of sex variations, 'Law and Contemporary Problems', 25, 292-308.
Brill, A.A. (1934), Homoerotism and paranoia, 'American Journal of Psychiatry', 90, 957-74.
Brown, Daniel G. (1957), The development of sex-role inversion and homo-sexuality, 'Journal of Pediatrics', 50, 613-19.
Bryan, Douglas (1930), Bisexuality, 'International Journal of Psycho-analysis', 11, 150-66.
Bychowski, Gustav (1930), A case of oral delusions of persecution, 'International

Journal of Psycho-analysis', 11, 332-7.
— (1945), The ego of homosexuals, 'International Journal of Psycho-analysis', 26, 114-27.
— (1954), The structure of homosexual acting out, 'Psychoanalytic Quarterly', 23, 48-61.
Cabeen, Charles W. and Coleman, James C. (1962), The selection of sex-offender patients for group psychotherapy, 'International Journal of Group Psychotherapy', 12, 326-34.
Cameron, John L., Freeman, Thomas and McGhie, Andrew (1956), Clinical observations on chronic schizophrenia, 'Psychiatry', 19, 271-81.
Cameron, Norman (1943a), The development of paranoic thinking, 'Psychological Review', 50, 219-33.
— (1943b), The paranoid pseudo-community, 'American Journal of Sociology', 49, 32-8.
— (1959a), The paranoid pseudo-community revisited, 'American Journal of Sociology', 65, 52-8.
— (1959b), Paranoid conditions and paranoia, in 'American Handbook of Psychiatry', Vol. 1, ed. Silvano Arieti, New York, Basic Books.
Cancro, R., Fox, N. and Shapiro, L.E. (eds) (1974), 'Strategic intervention in schizophrenia', New York, Behavioral Publications.
Caprio, Frank S. (1960), 'Female homosexuality', London, Peter Owen.
Carpenter, Edward (1909), 'The intermediate sex', London, Swan Sonnenschein, Manchester, S. Clarke.
Carr, Arthur C. (1963), Observations on paranoia, and their relationship to the Schreber case, 'International Journal of Psycho-analysis', 44, 195-200.
Cauldwell, D.O. (1949), Psychopathia transexualis, 'Sexology', 16, 274-80.
Clarke, A.D.B. and Clarke, Ann M. (1960), Some recent advances in the study of early deprivation, 'Journal of Child Psychology and Psychiatry', 1, 26-36.
Clarke, Murray, et al. (1954), Adrenogenital syndrome, 'Medical Journal of Australia', 2, 567-70.
Cleveland, Sidney E. (1956), Three cases of self-castration, 'Journal of Nervous and Mental Disease', 123, 386-91.
Coleman, Rose W. and Provence, Sally (1957), Environmental retardation (hospitalism) in infants living in families, 'Pediatrics', 19, 285-92.
Cowell, Roberta (1954), 'Roberta Cowell's Story'. London, Heinemann.
Cox, F.N. (1953), The origins of the dependency drive, 'Australian Journal of Psychology', 5, 64-75.
Creak, Mildred et al. (1961), Schizophrenic syndrome in childhood, 'Cerebral Palsy Bulletin', 3, 501-4.
Crowcroft, Andrew (1967), 'The psychotic', Harmondsworth, Penguin.
Cull, John (1971), Conformity behavior in schizophrenics, 'Journal of Social Psychology', 84, 45-9.
Dank, Barry M. (1971), Six homosexual siblings, 'Archives of Sexual Behavior', 1, 193-204.
Darke, Roy A. (1948), Heredity as an etiological factor in homosexuality, 'Journal of Nervous and Mental Disease', 107, 251-68.
Davidson, P. Waverly (1966), Transsexualism in Klinefelter's syndrome, 'Psychosomatics', 7, 94-8.
Deisher, Robert W., Eisner, Victor and Sulzbacher, Stephen I. (1969), The young male prostitute, 'Pediatrics', 43, 936-41.
Delay, J. Deniker, P., Volmat, R. and Alby, J.-M. (1956), Une demande de changement de sexe: le transsexualisme, 'Encephale', 45, 41-80.
Denford, J.D. (1967), The psychodynamics of homosexuality, 'New Zealand Medical Journal', 66, 743-4.
Dennis, Wayne (1938), Infant development under conditions of restricted practice and of minimum social stimulation: a preliminary report, 'Journal of Genetic Psychology', 53, 149-57.
Despert, J. Louise and Sherwin, Albert C. (1958), Further examination of diagnostic criteria in schizophrenic illness and psychoses of infancy and early childhood, 'American Journal of Psychiatry', 114, 784-90.
Despert, J. Louise (1971), Reflections on early infantile autism, 'Journal of

Autism and Childhood Schizophrenia', 1, 363-7.
Deutsch, Helene (1932), 'Homosexuality in women', 'Psychoanalytic Quarterly',
    1, 484-510.
— (1937), Absence of grief, 'Psychoanalytic Quarterly', 6, 12-22.
— (1938), Folie à deux, 'Psychoanalytic Quarterly', 7, 307-18.
Dewhurst, C.J. and Gordon, R.R. (1963), Change of sex, 'Lancet', 2, 1213-16.
Don, Alexander M. (1963) Transvestism and transsexualism, 'South African
    Medical Journal', 37, 479-85.
Dorey, R. (1956), L'inversion psycho-sexuelle avec travestissement chez
    l'homme, 'Semaine des Hopitaux', 32, 2667-73.
Druss, Richard G. (1967), Cases of suspected homosexuality seen at an army
    mental hygiene consultation service, 'Psychiatric Quarterly', 41, 62-70.
Du Pan, R. Martin and Roth, S. (1955), The psychologic development of a
    group of children brought up in a hospital type residential nursery, 'Journal
    of Pediatrics', 47, 124-9.
Editorial (1966), Transsexuality, 'British Medical Journal', 1, 873-4.
Ehrenwald, J. (1960), The symbiotic matrix of paranoid delusions and the
    homosexual alternative, 'American Journal of Psychoanalysis', 20, 49-65.
Ehrhardt, Anke A., Epstein, Ralph and Money, John (1968), Fetal androgens
    and female gender identity in the early-treated adrenogenital syndrome,
    'Johns Hopkins Medical Journal', 122, 160-7.
Eidelberg, Ludwig (1954), Neurosis, a negative of perversion?, 'Psychiatric
    Quarterly', 28, 607-12.
Elkisch, Paula and Mahler, Margaret S. (1959), On infantile precursors of the
    'influencing machine', 'Psychoanalytic Study of the Child', 14, 219-35.
Ellis, A. (1945), The sexual psychology of human hermaphrodites, 'Psycho-
    somatic Medicine', 7, 108-25.
Ellis, Havelock (1913), Sexo-aesthetic inversion, 'Alienist and Neurologist',
    34, 156-67.
— (1924), 'Sexual inversion', Philadelphia, F.A. Davis.
— (1928), 'Eonism', Philadelphia, F.A. Davis.
Ellison, E. Alden and Hamilton, Donald M. (1949), The hospital treatment of
    dementia praecox, 'American Journal of Psychiatry', 106, 454-61.
Esman, Aaron H. (1954), A case of self-castration, 'Journal of Nervous and
    Mental Disease', 120, 79-82.
— (1960), 'Childhood psychosis' and 'childhood schizophrenia', 'American
    Journal of Orthopsychiatry', 30, 391-6.
Esterson, Aaron (1972), 'The leaves of spring (Schizophrenia, family and
    sacrifice)', Harmondsworth, Penguin.
Evans, William N. (1951), Simulated pregnancy in a male, 'Psychoanalytic
    Quarterly', 20, 165-78.
Eyres, Alfred E. (1960), Transvestitism, 'Diseases of the Nervous System',
    21, 52-3.
Faergeman, Poul M. (1955), Fantasies of menstruation in men, 'Psychoanalytic
    Quarterly', 24, 1-19.
Fairbairn, W. Ronald D. (1952), 'Psychoanalytic studies of the personality',
    London, Tavistock.
— (1956), Considerations arising out of the Schreber case, 'British Journal of
    Medical Psychology', 29, 113-27.
— (1964), A note on the origin of male homosexuality, 'British Journal of
    Medical Psychology', 37, 31-2.
Fenichel, Otto (1930), The psychology of transvestism, 'International Journal
    of Psycho-analysis', 11: 211-27.
— (1945a), 'The psychoanalytic theory of neurosis', London, Routledge & Kegan
    Paul.
— (1945b), The concept of trauma in contemporary psycho-analytic theory,
    'International Journal of Psycho-analysis', 26, 33-44.
Ferenczi, S. (1950), (first published 1916) 'Sex in psychoanalysis', New York,
    Robert Brunner.
Field, L.H. and Williams, Mark (1970), The hormonal treatment of sexual
    offenders, 'Medicine, Science and the Law', 10, 27-34.

Fine, Roswell H. (1960), Apparent homosexuality in the adolescent girl, 'Diseases of the Nervous System', 21, 634-7.

Fleming, Joan (1972), Early object deprivation and transference phenomena: the working alliance, 'Psychoanalytic Quarterly', 41, 23-49.

Fluker, J.L. (1966), Recent trends in homosexuality in West London, 'British Journal of Venereal Diseases', 42, 48-9.

Fogh-Andersen, Poul (1956), Transvestism and trans-sexualism. Surgical treatment in a case of auto-castration, 'Acta Medicinae Legalis et Socialis', 9, 33-40.

Fookes, B.H. (1969), Some experiences in the use of aversion therapy in male homosexuality, exhibitionism and fetishism-transvestism, 'British Journal of Psychiatry', 115, 339-41.

Ford, Clellan S. (1960), Sex offenses: an anthropological perspective, 'Law and Contemporary Problems', 25, 225-43.

Ford, Clellan S. and Beach, Frank A. (1965), 'Patterns of sexual behavior', London, Methuen.

Fortineau, J., Vercier, R., Durand, Charles and Vidart, L. (1939), Idées de transformation sexuelle et travestissement chez deux délirants chroniques, 'Annales medico-psychologiques', 97, 51-5.

Foulkes, S.H. (1943), The idea of a change of sex in women', 'International Journal of Psycho-analysis', 24, 53-6.

Freeman, Thomas (1955), Clinical and theoretical observations on male homosexuality, 'International Journal of Psychoanalysis', 36, 335-47.

Freud, Anna (1950), 'The psycho-analytical treatment of children', London, Imago.

Freud, Anna and Burlingham, Dorothy (1974), 'Infants without families, and reports on the Hampstead Nurseries, 1939-1945', London, Hogarth Press.

Freud, Sigmund (1894), The neuro-psychoses of defence, Standard Edition, III.

— (1895 [1894]), Obsessions and phobias: their psychical mechanism and their aetiology, SE, III.

— (1898a), Sexuality in the aetiology of the neuroses, SE, III.

— (1898b), The psychical mechanism of forgetfulness, SE, III.

— (1905), Three essays on the theory of sexuality, SE, VII.

— (1910 [1909]), Five lectures on psycho-analysis, SE, XI.

— (1911), Psycho-analytic notes on an autobiographical account of a case of paranoia (dementia paranoides), SE, XII.

— (1912), The dynamics of transference, SE, XII.

— (1914a). Remembering, repeating and working-through, SE, XII.

— (1915 [1914]), Observations on transference-love, SE, XII.

— (1914b), On narcissism: an introduction, SE, XIV.

— (1915a), Instincts and their vicissitudes, SE, XIV.

— (1915b), Repression, SE, XIV.

— (1915c), A case of paranoia running counter to the psycho-analytic theory of the disease, SE, XIV.

— (1917 [1915]). Mourning and melancholia, SE, XIV.

— (1916-1917 [1915-1917]), Introductory lectures on psycho-analysis, Parts I and II, SE, XV.

— (1917 [1916-1917]), Introductory lectures on psycho-analysis, Part III, SE, XVI.

— (1918 [1914]), From the history of an infantile neurosis, SE, XVII.

— (1919), A child is being beaten, SE, XVII.

— (1920a), The psychogenesis of a case of homosexuality in a woman, SE, XVIII.

— (1920b), Beyond the pleasure principle, SE, XVIII.

— (1922), Some neurotic mechanisms in jealousy, paranoia and homosexuality, SE XVIII.

— (1923), The ego and the id, SE, XIX.

— (1924 [1923]), Neurosis and psychosis, SE, XIX.

— (1924a), The loss of reality in neurosis and psychosis, SE, XIX.

— (1924b), The dissolution of the Oedipus complex, SE, XIX.

— (1925), Some psychical consequences of the anatomical distinction between the sexes, SE, XIX.
— (1926 [1925]), Inhibitions, symptoms and anxiety, SE, XX.
— (1931), Female sexuality, SE, XXI.
— (1933 [1932]), New introductory lectures on psycho-analysis, SE, XXII.
— (1937a), Constructions in analysis, SE, XXIII.
— (1937b), Analysis terminable and interminable, SE, XXIII.
— (1940 [1938]), Splitting of the ego in the process of defence, SE, XXIII.
Freyhan, Fritz A. (1958), Eugen Bleuler's concept of the group of schizo-phrenias at mid-century, 'American Journal of Psychiatry', 114, 769-79.
Friend, Maurice R., Schiddel, Louise, Klein, Betty and Dunaeff, Dorothy (1954), Observations on the development of transvestitism in boys, 'American Journal of Orthopsychiatry', 24, 563-75.
Fromm-Reichmann, Frieda (1953), 'Principles of intensive psychotherapy', London, Allen & Unwin.
— (1958), Basic problems in the psychotherapy of schizophrenia, 'Psychiatry', 21, 1-6.
Furman, Robert A. (1964), Death and the young child, 'Psychoanalytic Study of the Child', 19, 321-33.
Gardiner, M. (ed.) (1972), 'The Wolf-Man and Sigmund Freud', London, Hogarth Press.
Geleerd, Elisabeth R. (1946), A contribution to the problem of psychosis in childhood, 'Psychoanalytic Study of the Child', 2, 271-91.
Giannell, A. Steven (1966), Giannell's criminosynthesis theory applied to female homosexuality, 'Journal of Psychology', 64, 213-22.
Gilbert, O.P. (1926), 'Men in women's guise', London, John Lane, The Bodley Head.
— (1932), 'Women in men's guise', London, John Lane, The Bodley Head.
Gillespie, W.H. (1952), Notes on the analysis of sexual perversions, 'International Journal of Psycho-analysis', 33, 397-402.
Gittleson, N.L. and Levine, S. (1966), Subjective ideas of sexual change in male schizophrenics, 'British Journal of Psychiatry', 112, 779-82.
Glaser, Kurt and Eisenberg, Leon (1956), Maternal deprivation, 'Pediatrics', 18, 626-42.
Glick, Burton, S. (1959), Homosexual panic: clinical and theoretical consider-ations, 'Journal of Nervous and Mental Disease', 129, 20-8.
Goffman, Erving (1973), !Stigma', Harmondsworth, Penguin.
Goldberg, G.J. (1965), Obsessional paranoid syndromes, 'Psychiatric Quarterly', 39, 43-64.
Goldberg, Philip A. and Milstein, Judith T. (1965), Perceptual investigation of psychoanalytic theory concerning latent homosexuality in women, 'Perceptual and Motor Skills', 21, 645-6.
Goldberg, Susan and Lewis, Michael (1969), Play behavior in the year-old infant: early sex differences, 'Child Development', 40, 21-31.
Goldfarb, William (1945), Effects of psychological deprivation in infancy and subsequent stimulation, 'American Journal of Psychiatry', 102, 18-33.
Goldrach, C. (1963), Deux cas de transsexualisme, 'Annales de Medecine Legale, de Criminologie et de Police Scientifique', 44, 64-71.
Golosow, N. and Weitzman, E.L. (1969), Psychosexual and ego regression in the male transsexual, 'Journal of Nervous and Mental Disease', 149, 328-36.
Grant, Vernon W. (1960), The cross-dresser: a case study, 'Journal of Nervous and Mental Disease', 131, 149-59.
Grauer, David (1955), Homosexuality and the paranoid psychoses as related to the concept of narcissism, 'Psychoanalytic Quarterly', 24, 516-26.
Green, André (1972), Aggression, femininity, paranoia and reality, 'International Journal of Psycho-analysis', 53, 205-11.
Green, David (1971), Legal aspects of transsexualism, 'Archives of Sexual Behavior', 1, 145-51.
Green, Richard (1968), Childhood cross-gender identification, 'Journal of Nervous and Mental Disease', 147, 500-9.
— (1971), Diagnosis and treatment of gender identity disorders during child-

hood, 'Archives of Sexual Behavior', 1, 167-73.
— (1972), Homosexuality as a mental illness, 'International Journal of
Psychiatry', 10, 77-98.
— (1974), 'Sexual identity conflict in children and adults', London, Duckworth.
— (1975), Sexual identity: research strategies, 'Archives of Sexual Behavior',
4, 337-52.
Green, R. and Money, J. (1960), Incongruous gender role: nongenital manifestations in prepubertal boys, 'Journal of Nervous and Mental Disease',
131, 160-8.
— (1966), Stage-acting, role-taking, and effeminate impersonation during
boyhood, 'Archives of General Psychiatry', 15, 535-8.
— (eds) (1969), 'Transsexualism and sex reassignment'. Baltimore, Johns
Hopkins Press.
Green R. and Stoller, R.J. (1971), Two monozygotic (identical) twin pairs dis-
cordant for gender identity, 'Archives of Sexual Behavior', 1, 321-7.
Green R., Stoller, R.J. and MacAndrew, Craig (1966a), Attitudes toward sex
transformation procedures, 'Archives of General Psychiatry', 15, 178-82.
— (1966b), Sex assignment and reassignment. Physicians' attitudes in the
management of hermaphroditic children, 'American Journal of Diseases of
Children', 111, 524-8.
Greenberg, Nahman H. and Rosenwald, Alan K. (1958), Transvestism and
pruritus perinei, 'Psychosomatic Medicine', 20, 145-50.
Greenberg, Nahman H., Rosenwald, Alan K. and Nielson, Paul E. (1960), A
study in transsexualism, 'Psychiatric Quarterly', 34, 203-35.
Greene, William A. (1958), Role of a vicarious object in the adaptation to object
loss, 'Psychosomatic Medicine', 20, 344-50.
Greenson, Ralph R. (1964), On homosexuality and gender identity, 'Inter-
national Journal of Psycho-analysis', 45, 217-19.
— (1966), A transvestite boy and a hypothesis, 'International Journal of
Psycho-analysis', 47, 396 403.
— (1968), Dis-identifying from mother: its special importance for the boy,
'International Journal of Psycho-analysis', 49, 370-4.
Grey, Antony (1975), Sexual law reform society working party report,
'Criminal Law Review', 323-35.
Grygier, Tadeusz (1958), Homosexuality, neurosis and 'normality'. A pilot
study in psychological measurement, 'British Journal of Delinquency', 9,
59-61.
Gundlach, Ralph H. and Riess, Bernard F. (1967), Birth order and sex of
siblings in a sample of lesbians and non-lesbians, 'Psychological Reports',
20, 61-2.
Gunther, Mavis (1955), Instinct and the nursing couple, 'Lancet', 1, 575-8.
Hadden, Samuel B. (1958), Treatment of homosexuality by individual and
group psychotherapy, 'American Journal of Psychiatry', 114, 810-15.
Haley, Jay (1960), Observation of the family of the schizophrenic, 'American
Journal of Orthopsychiatry', 30, 460-7.
Hamburger, Christian (1953), The desire for change of sex as shown by
personal letters from 465 men and women, 'Acta Endocrinologica', 14, 361-75.
Hamburger, Christian, Sturup, Georg K. and Dahl-Iversen, E. (1953),
Transvestism: hormonal, psychiatric and surgical treatment, 'Journal of the
American Medical Association', 152, 391-6.
Hamilton, Max (ed.) (1976), 'Fish's Schizophrenia', Bristol, John Wright.
Hampson, John L., Hampson, Joan G. and Money, John (1955), The syndrome
of gonadal agenesis (ovarian agenesis) and male chromosomal pattern in
girls and women: psychologic studies, 'Bulletin of the Johns Hopkins
Hospital', 97, 207-26.
Hastings, Donald W. (1941), A paranoid reaction with manifest homosexuality,
'Archives of Neurology and Psychiatry', 45, 379-81.
Haynes, Stephen N. (1970), Learning theory and the treatment of homo-
sexuality, 'Psychotherapy: theory, research and practice', 7, 91-4.
Hayward, Malcolm L. (1960), Schizophrenia and the double bind, 'Psychiatric
Quarterly', 34, 89-91.

Heiman, Elliott M. and Le, Cao Van (1975), Transsexualism in Vietnam, 'Archives of Sexual Behavior', 4, 89-95.

Hellman, Ilse (1962), Sudden separation and its effect followed over twenty years, 'Psychoanalytic Study of the Child', 17, 159-74.

Henderson, D.K. and Gillespie, R.D. (1975), 'Textbook of Psychiatry', London, Oxford University Press.

Henry, George W. (1939), A case of transvestitism, 'Journal of Nervous and Mental Disease', 89, 73-5.

— (1950), 'Sex Variants', London, Cassell.

Hertz, John, Tillinger, Karl-Gunnar and Westman, Axel (1961), Transvestitism: report on five hormonally and surgically treated cases, 'Acta Psychiatrica Scandinavica', 37, 283-94.

Hirsch, Steven R. and Leff, Julian P. (1975), 'Abnormalities in parents of schizophrenics', London, Oxford University Press.

Hirschfeld, Magnus (1937), 'Sexual anomalies and perversions', London, Francis Aldor.

Hoch, Paul H. (1957), The etiology and epidemiology of schizophrenia, 'American Journal of Public Health', 47, 1071-6.

Hoch, Paul and Polatin, Phillip (1949), Pseudoneurotic forms of schizophrenia, 'Psychiatric Quarterly', 23, 248-76.

Hoedemaker, Edward D. (1958), Preanalytic preparation for the therapeutic process in schizophrenia, 'Psychiatry', 21, 285-91.

Hoenig, J. and Kenna, J. (1974), The prevalence of transsexualism in England and Wales, 'British Journal of Psychiatry', 124, 181-90.

Hoenig, J., Kenna, J. and Youd, Ann, (1970a), Social and economic aspects of transsexualism, 'British Journal of Psychiatry', 117, 163-72.

— (1970b), A follow-up study of transsexualists: social and economic aspects, 'Psychiatria Clinica', 3, 85-100.

Hoffer, W. (1956), Transference and transference neurosis, 'International Journal of Psycho-analysis', 37, 377-9.

Holemon, R.E. and Winokur, G. (1965), Effeminate homosexuality: a disease of childhood, 'American Journal of Orthopsychiatry', 35, 48-56.

Hoopes, John E., Knorr, Norman J. and Wolf, Sanford, R. (1968), 'Transsexualism: considerations regarding sexual reassignment: 'Journal of Nervous and Mental Disease', 147, 510-16.

Hopkin, June H. (1969), The lesbian personality, 'British Journal of Psychiatry', 115, 1433-6.

Hora, Thomas (1953), The structural analysis of transvestitism, 'Psychoanalytic Review', 40, 268-74.

Hore, B.D., Nicolle, F.V. and Calnan, J.S. (1975), Male transsexualism in England: sixteen cases with surgical intervention, 'Archives of Sexual Behavior', 4, 81-8.

Horney, Karen (1926), The flight from womanhood, 'International Journal of Psycho-analysis', 7, 324-39.

Horton, C.B. and Clarke, Eric Kent (1931), Transvestism or eonism, 'American Journal of Psychiatry', 87, 1025-1030.

Horwitz, William A., Polatin, Philip, Kolb, Lawrence C. and Hoch, Paul H. (1958), A study of cases of schizophrenia treated by 'direct analysis', 'American Journal of Psychiatry', 114, 780-3.

Howells, J.G. and Layng, J. (1955), Separation experiences and mental health, 'Lancet', 2, 285-8.

Hoyer, Niels (ed.) (1933), 'Man into woman', London, Jarrolds.

Hynie, Josef (1978), The stress factor in sexual inadequacy, in 'Society, Stress and Disease', Vol. 3: 'The productive and reproductive age - male/female roles and relationships', ed. Lennart Levi, London, Oxford University Press.

Ionescu, B., Maximilian, C. and Bucur, A. (1971), Two cases of transsexualism with gonadal dysgenesia, 'British Journal of Psychiatry', 119, 311-4.

Jackson, Katherine, Winkley, Ruth, Faust, Otto A. and Cermak, Ethel G. (1952), Problems of emotional trauma in hospital treatment of children, 'Journal of the American Medical Association', 149, 1536-8.

Jacobson, Edith (1950), Development of the wish for a child in boys, 'Psycho-

analytic Study of the Child', 5, 139-52.
James, B. (1967a), Learning theory and homosexuality, 'New Zealand Medical Journal', 66, 748-51.
— (1967b), Behaviour therapy applied to homosexuality, 'New Zealand Medical Journal', 66, 752-4.
Jefferiss, F.J.G. (1966), Homosexually acquired venereal disease, 'British Journal of Venereal Diseases', 42, 46-7.
Johnson, Adelaide M., Giffin, Mary E., Watson, E. Jane and Beckett, Peter G.S. (1956), Observations on ego functions in schizophrenia, 'Psychiatry', 19, 143-8.
Jones, Ernest (1927), The early development of female sexuality, 'International Journal of Psycho-analysis', 8, 459-72.
Jones, Howard W. and Verkauf, Barry S. (1970), Surgical treatment in congenital adrenal hyperplasia, 'Journal of Obstetrics and Gynecology', 36, 1-10.
Jones, Maxwell et al. (1952), 'Social Psychiatry', London, Tavistock.
Jorgensen, Christine (1973), 'Christine Jorgensen', New York, Bantam Books.
Jung, C.G. (1907), Analysis of a case of paranoid dementia as a paradigm, in 'The psychogenesis of mental disease' (1977), London, Routledge & Kegan Paul.
Kallmann, Franz J. (1952), Comparative twin study on the genetic aspects of male homosexuality, 'Journal of Nervous and Mental Disease', 115, 283-98.
Kando, Thomas (1973), 'Sex change'. Springfield, Illinois, Charles C. Thomas.
Kanner, Leo (1944), Early infantile autism, 'Journal of Pediatrics', 25, 211-17.
— (1971), Childhood psychosis: a historical overview, 'Journal of Autism and Childhood Schizophrenia', 1, 14-19.
Kaplan, Harold I. and Sadock, Benjamin J. (1971), Recent perspectives in schizophrenia, 'Canadian Psychiatric Association Journal', 16, 457-71.
Karon, Bertram P. and Rosberg, Jack (1958), The homosexual urges in schizophrenia, 'Psychoanalytic Review', 45, 50-6.
Karpman, Ben (1943), Mediate psychotherapy and the acute homosexual panic (Kempf's disease), 'Journal of Nervous and Mental Disease', 98, 493-506.
Katan, M. (1939), A contribution to the understanding of schizophrenic speech, 'International Journal of Psycho-analysis', 20, 353-62.
— (1949), Schreber's delusion of the end of the world, 'Psychoanalytic Quarterly', 18, 60-6.
— (1950), Schreber's hallucinations about the 'little men', 'International Journal of Psycho-analysis', 31, 32-5.
— (1952), Further remarks about Schreber's hallucinations, 'International Journal of Psycho-analysis', 33, 429-32.
— (1953), Schreber's prepsychotic phase, 'International Journal of Psycho-analysis', 34, 43-51.
— (1959), Schreber's hereafter, 'Psychoanalytic Study of the Child', 14, 314-382.
— (1974), The development of the influencing apparatus, 'Psychoanalytic Study of the Child', 29, 473-510.
Katkin, Steven, Ginsburg, Marshall, Rifkin, Marilyn J. and Scott, James T. (1971), Effectiveness of female volunteers in the treatment of outpatients, 'Journal of Counseling Psychology', 18, 97-100.
Kaufman, M. Ralph (1934), Projection, heterosexual and homosexual, 'Psychoanalytic Quarterly', 3, 134-6.
— (1939), Religious delusions in schizophrenia, 'International Journal of Psycho-analysis', 20, 363-76.
Kenyon, F.E. (1968a), Studies in female homosexuality; social and psychiatric aspects, 'British Journal of Psychiatry', 114, 1337-50.
— (1968b), Studies in female homosexuality: psychological test results, 'Journal of Consulting and Clinical Psychology', 32, 510-13.
— (1970), Homosexuality in the female, 'British Journal of Hospital Medicine', 3, 183-206.
Kinross-Wright, Vernon and Kahn, Eugen (1958), Of schizophrenia and the schizophrenic, 'American Journal of Psychiatry', 114, 703-6.
Kinsey, Alfred C., Pomeroy, Wardell B. and Martin, Clyde E. (1953a), 'Sexual

behavior in the human male', Philadelphia and London, W.B. Saunders.

Kinsey, Alfred C., Pomeroy, Wardell B., Martin, Cylde E. and Gebhard, Paul H. (1953b), 'Sexual behavior in the human female'. Philadelphia and London, W.B. Saunders.

Kitay, Philip M. (1963), Symposium on reinterpretations of the Schreber case: Introduction + Note + Summary, 'International Journal of Psycho-analysis', 44, 191-4, 207, 222-3.

Klaf, Franklin S. and Davis, Charles A. (1960), Homosexuality and paranoid schizophrenia, 'American Journal of Psychiatry', 116: 1070-5.

Klaf, Franklin S. (1961), Female homosexuality and paranoid schizophrenia, 'Archives of General Psychiatry', 4, 84-6.

Kleeman, James A. (1971a), The establishment of core gender identity in normal girls. I. (a) Introduction; (b) Development of the ego capacity to differentiate, 'Archives of Sexual Behavior', 1, 103-16.

— (1971b), The establishment of core gender identity in normal girls. II. How meanings are conveyed between parent and child in the first three years, 'Archives of Sexual Behavior', 1, 117-29.

Klein, H.R. and Horwitz, W.A. (1949), Psychosexual factors in the paranoid phenomena, 'American Journal of Psychiatry', 105, 697-701.

Klein, Melanie, Heimann, Paula, Isaacs, Susan and Riviere, Joan (1952), 'Developments in psycho-analysis', London, Hogarth Press.

Knight, Robert P. (1940), The relationship of latent homosexuality to the mechanism of paranoid delusions. 'Bulletin of the Menninger Clinic', 4, 149-59.

Knorr, Norman J., Wolf, Sanford R. and Meyer, Eugene (1968), The trans-sexual's request for surgery, 'Journal of Nervous and Mental Disease', 147, 517-24.

Kolb, Lawrence C. (1959) Disturbances of the body-image, in 'American Handbook of Psychiatry', Vol. 1, ed. Silvano Arieti. New York, Basic Books.

Kolb, Lawrence C. and Johnson, Adelaide M. (1955), Etiology and therapy of overt homosexuality, 'Psychoanalytic Quarterly', 24, 506-15.

Kraemer, William (ed.) (1976), 'The forbidden love', London, Sheldon Press.

Kraepelin, Emil (1921), 'Manic-depressive insanity and paranoia', Edinburgh, Livingstone.

Krafft-Ebing, Richard Von (1939) (first published 1899), 'Psychopathia sexualis', London, Heinemann.

Kremer, M.W. and Rifkin, A.H. (1969), The early development of homosexuality: a study of adolescent lesbians, 'American Journal of Psychiatry', 126, 91-6.

Kubie, L.S. and Mackie, J.B. (1968), Critical issues raised by operations for gender transmutation, 'Journal of Nervous and Mental Disease', 147, 431-43.

Lafitte, Francois (1958), Homosexuality and the law, 'British Journal of Delinquency', 9, 8-19.

Laforgue, Rene (1927), Scotomization in schizophrenia, 'International Journal of Psycho-analysis', 8, 473-8.

Lagache, Daniel (1950), Homosexuality and jealousy, 'International Journal of Psycho-analysis', 31, 24-31.

Laing, R.D. (1964), Is schizophrenia a disease?, 'International Journal of Social Psychiatry', 10, 184-93.

— (1965), 'The divided self', Harmondsworth, Penguin.

— (1976a), 'Self and others'. Harmondsworth, Penguin.

— (1976b), 'The politics of the family', Harmondsworth, Penguin.

Laing, R.D. and Esterson, A. (1964), 'Sanity, madness and the family', London, Tavistock.

Lake, Frank (1966), 'Clinical theology', London, Darton, Longman & Todd.

Langford, William S. (1948), Physical illness and convalescence: their meaning to the child, 'Journal of Pediatrics', 33, 242-50.

Laufer, Berthold (1920), Sex transformation and hermaphrodites in China, 'American Journal of Physical Anthropology', 3, 259-62.

Lester, David (1975), The relationship between paranoid delusions and homosexuality, 'Archives of Sexual Behavior', 4, 285-94.

Levy, David M. (1937), Primary affect hunger, 'American Journal of Psychiatry', 94, 643-52.

Lewinsky, Hilde (1949), Notes on two special features in a homosexual patient, 'International Journal of Psycho-analysis', 30, 56.

Lewis, Aubrey (1970), Paranoia and paranoid: a historical perspective, 'Psychological Medicine', 1, 2-12.

Lewis, Michael (1975), Early sex differences in the human: studies of socio-emotional development, 'Archives of Sexual Behavior', 4, 329-35.

Lewis, Murray D. (1963), A case of transvestism with multiple body-phallus identification, 'International Journal of Psycho-analysis', 44, 345-51.

Lewis, Viola G., Ehrhardt, Anke A. and Money, John (1970), Genital operations in girls with the adrenogenital syndrome: subsequent psychologic development, 'Journal of Obstetrics and Gynecology', 36, 11-15.

Lichtenstein, Heinz (1961), Identity and sexuality, 'Journal of the American Psychoanalytic Association', 9, 179-260.

Lidz, R.W. and Lidz, T. (1969), Homosexual tendencies in mothers of schizophrenic women, 'Journal of Nervous and Mental Disease', 149, 229-35.

Lidz, Theodore (1958), Schizophrenia and the family, 'Psychiatry', 21, 21-7.

— (1975), 'The origin and treatment of schizophrenic disorders', London, Hutchinson.

Lidz, Theodore, Parker, Beulah and Cornelison, Alice (1956), The role of the father in the family environment of the schizophrenic patient, 'American Journal of Psychiatry', 113, 126-32.

Lidz, Theodore, Wild, Cynthia, Schafer, Sarah, Rosman, Bernice and Fleck, Stephen (1963), Thought disorders in the parents of schizophrenic patients: a study utilizing the object sorting test, 'Journal of Psychiatric Research', 1, 193-200.

Liebman, Samuel (1944) Homosexuality, transvestism, and psychosis, 'Journal of Nervous and Mental Disease', 99, 945-58.

Lief, Harold I., Dingman, Joseph F. and Bishop, Melvin P. (1962), Psycho-endocrinologic studies in a male with cyclic changes in sexuality, 'Psychosomatic Medicine', 24, 357-68.

Limentani, Davide (1956), Symbiotic identification in schizophrenia, 'Psychiatry', 19, 231-6.

Lindemann, Erich (1944), Symptomatology and management of acute grief, 'American Journal of Psychiatry', 101, 141-8.

Litman, Robert E. and Swearingen, Charles (1972), Bondage and suicide, 'Archives of General Psychiatry', 27, 80-5.

Lorand, A.S. (1930), Fetishism in statu nascendi, 'International Journal of Psycho-analysis', 11, 419-27.

— (1939), Role of the female penis phantasy in male character formation, 'International Journal of Psycho-analysis', 20, 171-82.

Lorand, A.S. and Balint, Michael (eds) (1965), 'Perversions: psychodynamics and therapy'. London, Ortolan Press.

Lowy, Frederick H. and Kolivakis, Thomas L. (1971), Autocastration by a male transsexual, 'Canadian Psychiatric Association Journal', 16, 399-405.

Lukianowicz, N. (1959a), Transvestism and psychosis, 'Psychiatria et Neurologia', 138, 64-78.

— (1959b), Survey of various aspects of transvestism in the light of our present knowledge, 'Journal of Nervous and Mental Disease', 128, 36-64.

— (1960), Two cases of transvestism, 'Psychiatric Quarterly', 34, 517-37.

— (1962), Transvestite episodes in acute schizophrenia, 'Psychiatric Quarterly', 36, 44-54.

— (1965), Symbolical self-strangulation in a transvestite schizophrenic, 'Psychiatric Quarterly', 39, 244-57.

Lurie, Abraham and Ron, Harold (1971), Multiple family group counseling of discharged schizophrenic young adults and their parents, 'Social Psychiatry', 6, 88-92.

Macalpine, Ida (1950), The development of the transference, 'Psychoanalytic Quarterly', 19, 501-39.

Macalpine, Ida and Hunter, Richard A. (1953), The Schreber case, 'Psychoanalytic Quarterly', 22, 328-71.

— (eds) (1955), 'Memoirs of my nervous illness, by Daniel Paul Schreber',

London, William Dawson.

McConaghy, N. (1969), Subjective and penile plethysmograph responses following aversion-relief and apomorphine aversion therapy for homosexual impulses, 'British Journal of Psychiatry', 115, 723-30.

McCullagh, E.P. and Renshaw, J.F. (1934), The effects of castration in the adult male, 'Journal of the American Medical Association', 103, 1140-3.

Mac Donough, Tomi S. (1972). A critique of the first Feldman and MacCulloch avoidance conditioning treatment for homosexuals, 'Behavior Therapy', 3, 104-11.

McGuire, Michael T. and Fairbanks, Lynn A. (1977), 'Ethological psychiatry', New York, Grune & Stratton.

Mac Keith, Ronald (1953), Children in hospital: preparation for operation, 'Lancet', 2, 843-5.

MacKenzie, D.F. (1967), Homosexuality and the justice department, 'New Zealand Medical Journal', 66, 745-8.

Maenchen, Anna (1953), Notes on early ego disturbances, 'Psychoanalytic Study of the Child', 8, 262-70.

Mahler, Margaret S. (1961), On sadness and grief in infancy and childhood, 'Psychoanalytic Study of the Child, 16, 332-51.

— (1969), 'Infantile psychosis', London, Hogarth Press.

Mahler, Margaret S. and Elkisch, Paula (1953), Some observations on disturbances of the ego in a case of infantile psychosis, 'Psychoanalytic Study of the Child', 8, 252-61.

Marks, Isaac, Gelder Michael and Bancroft, John (1970), Sexual deviants two years after electric aversion, 'British Journal of Psychiatry', 117, 173-85.

Marmor, Judd (1972), Homosexuality - mental illness or moral dilemma?, 'International Journal of Psychiatry', 10, 114-17.

Martensen-Larsen, O. (1957), The family constellation and homosexualism, 'Acta Genetica et Statistica Medica', 7, 445-6.

Martin, Barclay (1973), 'Abnormal psychology', Glenview, Illinois, Scott, Foresman & Co.

Mayer-Gross, W., Slater, E. and Roth, M. (1969), 'Clinical Psychiatry', London, Bailliere Tindall.

Meyer, Jon K., Knorr, Norman J. and Blumer, Dietrich (1971), Characterization of a self-designated transsexual population, 'Archives of Sexual Behavior', 1, 219-30.

Meyers, David William (1968), Problems of sex determination and alteration, 'Medico-legal Journal', 36, 174-90.

Miller, Charles W. (1941), The paranoid syndrome, 'Archives of Neurology and Psychiatry', 45, 953-63.

— (1942), Factors affecting the prognosis of paranoid disorders, 'Journal of Nervous and Mental Disease', 95, 580-8.

Miller, D.H., Clancy, J. and Cumming, E. (1953), A method of evaluating progress in patients suffering from chronic schizophrenia, 'Psychiatric Quarterly', 27, 439-51.

Miller, Milton L. (1942), A psychological study of a case of eczema and a case of neurodermatitis, 'Psychosomatic Medicine', 4, 82-93.

Mishler, Elliot G. and Waxler, Nancy E. (1965), Family interaction processes and schizophrenia: a review of current theories, 'Merrill-Palmer Quarterly of Behavior and Development', 11, 269-315.

— (1970), Functions of hesitations in the speech of normal families and families of schizophrenic patients, 'Language and Speech', 13, 102-17.

Modlin, Herbert C. (1963), Psychodynamics and management of paranoid states in women, 'Archives of General Psychiatry', 8, 263-8.

Monchy, Rene de (1965), A clinical type of male homosexuality, 'International Journal of Psycho-analysis', 46, 218-25.

Moncrieff, Alan and Walton, A.M. (1952), Visiting children in hospital, 'British Medical Journal', 1, 43-4.

Money, John (1971), Prefatory remarks on outcome of sex reassignment in 24 cases of transsexualism, 'Archives of Sexual Behavior', 1, 163-5.

Money, John and Brennan, John G. (1968), Sexual dimorphism in the psychology of female transsexuals, 'Journal of Nervous and Mental Disease', 147, 487-99.

Money, John and Primrose, Clay (1968), Sexual dimorphism and dissociation in the psychology of male transsexuals, 'Journal of Nervous and Mental Disease', 147, 472-86.

Money, John and Wolff, George (1973), Sex reassignment: male to female to male, 'Archives of Sexual Behavior', 2, 245-50.

Money, John, Hampson, Joan G. and Hampson, John L. (1955a), Hermaphroditism: recommendations concerning assignment of sex, change of sex, and psychologic management, 'Bulletin of the Johns Hopkins Hospital', 97, 284-300.

— (1955b), An examination of some basic sexual concepts: the evidence of human hermaphroditism, 'Bulletin of the Johns Hopkins Hospital', 97, 301-19.

— (1957), Imprinting and the establishment of gender role, 'Archives of Neurology and Psychiatry', 77, 333-6.

Moore, Robert A. and Selzer, Melvin L. (1963), Male homosexuality, paranoia, and the schizophrenias, 'American Journal of Psychiatry', 119, 743-7.

Morris, J. (1974), 'Conundrum', London, Faber & Faber.

Mosier, H. David and Goodwin, Willard E. (1961), Feminizing adrenal adenoma in a seven-year-old boy, 'Pediatrics', 27, 1016-21.

Mosse, Hilde L. (1958), The misuse of the diagnosis childhood schizophrenia, 'American Journal of Psychiatry', 114, 791-4.

Munroe, Robert L. and Munroe, Ruth H. (1971), Male pregnancy symptoms and cross-sex identity in three societies, 'Journal of Social Psychology', 84, 11-25.

Mussen, Paul and Distler, Luther (1959), Masculinity, identification, and father-son relationships, 'Journal of Abnormal and Social Psychology', 59, 350-6.

Nedoma, Karel (1951), Homosexuality in sexological practice, 'International Journal of Sexology', 4, 219-24.

Neustatter, W. Lindesay (1954), Homosexuality: the medical aspect, 'Practitioner', 172, 364-73.

— (1961), Sexual abnormalities and the sexual offender, 'Medico-legal Journal', 29, 190-9.

Niederland, William G. (1951), Three notes on the Schreber case, 'Psychoanalytic Quarterly', 20, 579-91.

— (1959), The 'miracled-up' world of Schreber's childhood, 'Psychoanalytic Study of the Child', 14, 383-413.

— (1963), Further data and memorabilia pertaining to the Schreber case, 'International Journal of Psycho-analysis', 44, 201-7.

— (1972), The Schreber case sixty years later, 'International Journal of Psychiatry', 10, 79-84.

Norman, Jacob P. (1948), Evidence and clinical significance of homosexuality in 100 unanalyzed cases of dementia praecox, 'Journal of Nervous and Mental Disease', 107, 484-9.

Norris, A.S. and Keettel, W.C. (1962), Change of sex-role during adolescence, 'American Journal of Obstetrics and Gynaecology', 84, 719-21.

Northrup, Gordon (1959), Transsexualism, 'Archives of General Psychiatry', 1, 332-7.

Nuffield, E.J.A. (1954), The schizogenic mother, 'Medical Journal of Australia', 2, 283-6.

Nunberg, H. (1938), Homosexuality, magic and aggression, 'International Journal of Psycho-analysis', 19, 1-16.

— (1951), Transference and reality, 'International Journal of Psychoanalysis', 32, 1-9.

Nydes, Jule (1963), Schreber, parricide, and paranoid-masochism, 'International Journal of Psycho-analysis', 44, 208-212.

Olkon, D.M. and Sherman, I.C. (1944), Eonism with added outstanding psychopathic features, 'Journal of Nervous and Mental Disease', 99, 159-67.

Ormrod, Roger (1975), Medicolegal aspects of sex determination, 'Forensic Science', 5, 1-9.

Ostow, Mortimer (1953), Transvestism, 'Journal of the American Medical Association', 152, 1553.

Ovesey, Lionel (1954), The homosexual conflict, 'Psychiatry', 17, 243-50.
— (1955a), The pseudohomosexual anxiety, 'Psychiatry', 18, 17-25.
— (1955b), 'Pseudohomosexuality, the paranoid mechanism, and paranoia, 'Psychiatry', 18, 163-73.
— (1956), Masculine aspirations in women, 'Psychiatry', 19, 341-51.
Ovesey, Lionel, Gaylin, Willard and Hendin, Herbert (1963), Psychotherapy of male homosexuality,' Archives of General Psychiatry', 9, 19-31.
Pardes, Herbert, Steinberg, Jorge and Simons, Richard C. (1967), A rare case of overt and mutual homosexuality in female identical twins, 'Psychiatric Quarterly', 41, 108-33.
Parker, William (1972), The homosexual in American society today: the homophile - gay liberation movement, 'Criminal Law Bulletin', 8, 692-9.
Parkes, Colin Murray (1975), 'Bereavement', Harmondsworth, Penguin.
Parr, Denis (1958), Psychiatric aspects of the Wolfenden report, II, 'British Journal of Delinquency', 9, 33-43.
Pauly, Ira B. (1965), Male psychosexual inversion: transsexualism, 'Archives of General Psychiatry', 13, 172-81.
— (1968), The current status of the change of sex operation, 'Journal of Nervous and Mental Disease', 147, 460-71.
Pauly, Ira B. (1969), Adult manifestations of female transsexualism, in Green and Money (eds), 'Transsexualism and Sex Reassignment'.
Peto, Endre (1949), Infant and mother: observations on object-relations in early infancy, 'International Journal of Psycho-analysis', 30, 260-64.
Philbert, M. (1971), Male transsexualism: an endocrine study, 'Archives of Sexual Behavior', 1, 91-3.
Philippopoulos, G.S. (1964), A case of transvestitism in a 17-year-old girl, 'Acta Psychotherapeutica, Psychosomatica et Orthopaedagogica', 12, 29-37.
Planansky, Karel and Johnston, Roy (1962), The incidence and relationship of homosexual and paranoid features in schizophrenia, 'Journal of Mental Science', 108, 604-615.
Ploscowe, Morris (1960), Sex offenses: the American legal context, 'Law and Contemporary Problems', 25, 217-24.
Podolsky, Edward (1952), The mind of the transvestite, 'International Journal of Sexology', 6, 107-8.
Pollock, George H. (1964), On symbiosis and symbotic neurosis, 'International Journal of Psycho-analysis', 45, 1-30.
Powers, Grover F. (1948), Humanizing hospital experiences, 'American Journal of Diseases of Children', 76, 365-79.
Pringle, M.L. Kellmer and Bossio, V. (1960), Early prolonged separation and emotional maladjustment, 'Journal of Child Psychology and Psychiatry', 1, 37-48.
Raboch, Jan and Nedoma, Karel (1958), Sex chromatin and sexual behavior, 'Psychosomatic Medicine', 20, 55-9.
Rado, Sandor (1940), A critical examination of the concept of bisexuality, 'Psychosomatic Medicine', 2, 459-67.
Ramsay, R.A., Ban, T.A., Lehmann, H.E., Saxena, B.M. and Bennett, Jean (1970), Nicotinic acid as adjuvant therapy in newly admitted schizophrenic patients, 'Canadian Medical Association Journal', 102, 939-42.
Randell, John B. (1959), Transvestism and trans-sexualism, 'British Medical Journal', 2, 1448-52.
— (1970), Transvestism and trans-sexualism, 'British Journal of Hospital Medicine', 3, 211-13.
— (1971), Indications for sex reassignment surgery, 'Archives of Sexual Behavior', 1, 153-161.
Ries, Hannah, (1945), An unwelcome child and her death instinct, 'International Journal of Psycho-analysis', 26, 153-61.
Robertson, Joyce, (1962), Mothering as an influence on early development, 'Psychoanalytic Study of the Child', 17, 245-64.
Rochlin, Gregory (1953), Loss and restitution, 'Psychoanalytic Study of the Child', 8, 288-309.
— (1961), The dread of abandonment, 'Psychoanalytic Study of the Child, 16, 451-70.

Roff, Merrill (1963), Childhood social interactions and young adult psychosis, 'Journal of Clinical Psychology', 19, 152-7.
Rogerson, C.H. (1937), The psychological factors in asthma-prurigo, 'Quarterly Journal of Medicine', 6, 367-94.
Romm, May E. (1957), Transient psychotic episodes during psychoanalysis, 'Journal of the American Psychoanalytic Association', 5, 325-41.
Rosen, David H. (1974), 'Lesbianism', Springfield, Illinois, Charles C. Thomas.
Rosenfeld, Herbert A. (1965), 'Psychotic states: a psycho-analytical approach', London, Hogarth Press.
Rubinstein, L.H. (1958), Psychotherapeutic aspects of male homosexuality, 'British Journal of Medical Psychology', 31, 14-18.
Ruitenbeek, Hendrik M. (ed.) (1963), 'The problem of homosexuality in modern society', New York, E.P. Dutton.
Rupp, Joseph C. (1970), Sudden death in the gay world, 'Medicine, Science and the Law', 10, 189-91.
Russell, Donald Hayes (1971), On the psychopathology of boy prostitutes, 'International Journal of Offender Therapy', 15, 49-52.
Sagarin, Edward and MacNamara, Donald E.J. (1970), The problem of entrapment, 'Crime and Delinquency', 16, 363-78.
Saghir, M.T. and Robins, Eli (1969), Homosexuality: sexual behavior of the female homosexual, 'Archives of General Psychiatry', 20, 192-201.
Saghir, M.T. and Robins, Eli (1971), Male and female homosexuality: natural history, 'Comprehensive Psychiatry', 12, 503-510.
Saghir, M.T., Robins, Eli, Walbran, Bonnie and Gentry, Kathye A. (1970a), Homosexuality: psychiatric disorders and disability in the male homosexual, 'American Journal of Psychiatry', 126, 1079-86.
— (1970b), Homosexuality: psychiatric disorders and disability in the female homosexual, 'American Journal of Psychiatry', 127, 147-54.
Santrock, John W. (1970), Paternal absence, sex typing, and identification, 'Developmental Psychology', 2, 264-72.
Saul, Leon J. (1938), Incidental observations on pruritus ani, 'Psychoanalytic Quarterly', 7, 336-7.
Savitsch, Eugene de (1958), 'Homosexuality, transvestism and change of sex', London, Heinemann Medical Books.
Schaffer, H.R. (1958), Objective observations of personality development in early infancy, 'British Journal of Medical Psychology', 31, 174-83.
Schaffer, H.R. and Callender, W.M. (1959), Psychologic effects of hospitalization in infancy, 'Pediatrics', 24, 528-39.
Scharl, Adele E. (1961), Regression and restitution in object loss, 'Psychoanalytic Study of the Child', 16, 471-80.
Schatzman, Morton (1972), 'Paranoia or persecution: the case of Schreber, 'International Journal of Psychiatry', 10, 53-78.
— (1973), 'Soul Murder', London, Allen Lane.
Scheflen, Albert E. (1960), Regressive one-to-one relationships, 'Psychiatric Quarterly', 34, 692-709.
Schmideberg, Melitta (1931), A contribution to the psychology of persecutory ideas and delusions, 'International Journal of Psycho-analysis', 12, 331-67.
Schneider, Stanley F., Harrison, Saul, I. and Siegel, Barry L. (1965), Self castration by a man with cyclic changes in sexuality, 'Psychosomatic Medicine', 27, 53-70.
Schopler, Eric and Reichler, Robert J. (1971), Parents as cotherapists in the treatment of psychotic children, 'Journal of Autism and Childhood Schizophrenia', 1, 87-102.
Schreber, D.G.M. (1899), 'Medical indoor gymnastics', London, Edinburgh and Oxford, Williams & Norgate.
Schreber, Daniel Paul (1955), 'Memoirs of my nervous illness', trans. and ed. by Ida Macalpine and Richard A. Hunter, London, William Dawson.
Schur, Edwin M. (1965), 'Crimes without victims', Englewood Cliffs, New Jersey, Prentice-Hall.
Schwartz, Bernard J. (1955), An empirical test of two Freudian hypotheses concerning castration anxiety, 'Journal of Personality', 24, 318-27.

Schwartz, D.A. (1963), A re-view of the 'paranoid' concept, 'Archives of General Psychiatry', 8, 349-61.

Scott, Peter D. (1958), Psychiatric aspects of the Wolfenden report, I, 'British Journal of Delinquency', 9, 20-32.

Searles, Harold F. (1965), 'Collected papers on schizophrenia and related subjects', London, Hogarth Press.

Segal, Morey M. (1965), Transvestitism as an impulse and as a defence, 'International Journal of Psycho-analysis', 46, 209-217.

Sendrail, Marcel and Gleizes, Leon (1961), Le trans-sexualisme feminin et le probleme de ses conditions psychiques ou hormonales, 'Revue Francaise d'Endocrinologie Clinique', 2, 35-44.

Seth, George and Beloff, Halla (1959), Language impairment in a group of schizophrenics, 'British Journal of Medical Psychology', 32, 288-93.

Sevringhaus, E.L. and Chornyak, John (1945), A study of homosexual adult males, 'Psychosomatic Medicine', 7, 302-5.

Shankel, L. Willard and Carr, Arthur C. (1956), Transvestism and hanging episodes in a male adolescent, 'Psychiatric Quarterly', 30, 478-93.

Sherfey, Mary Jane (1966), The evolution and nature of female sexuality in relation to psychoanalytic theory, 'Journal of the American Psychoanalytic Association', 14, 28-128.

Shevin, Frederick F. (1963) Counter-transference and identity phenomena manifested in the analysis of a case of 'phallus girl' identity, 'Journal of the American Psychoanalytic Association', 11, 331-44.

Shields, Robert W. (1964), The too-good mother, 'International Journal of Psycho-analysis', 45, 85-8.

Simon, Robert I. (1967), A case of female transsexualism, 'American Journal of Psychiatry', 123, 1598-601.

Singer, M.T. and Wynne, L.C. (1965a), Thought disorder and family relations of schizophrenics: methodology using projective techniques, 'Archives of General Psychiatry', 12, 187-200.

— (1965b), Thought disorder and family relations of schizophrenics: results and implications, 'Archives of General Psychiatry', 12, 201-12.

Singer, Melvin and Fischer, Ruth (1967), Group psychotherapy of male homosexuals by a male and female co-therapy team, 'International Journal of Group Psychotherapy', 17, 44-52.

Slater, Eliot and Slater, Patrick (1947), A study in the assessment of homosexual traits, 'British Journal of Medical Psychology', 21, 61-74.

Smith, Charles E. (1954), The homosexual federal offender: a study of 100 cases, 'Journal of Criminal Law, Criminology and Police Science', 44, 582-91.

Smitt, Jarl Wagner (1952), Homosexuality in a new light, 'International Journal of Sexology', 6, 36-9.

Socarides, C.W. (1963), The historical development of theoretical and clinical concepts of overt female homosexuality, 'Journal of the American Psychoanalytic Association', 11, 386-414.

— (1968a), 'The overt homosexual', New York and London, Grune & Stratton.

— (1968b), A provisional theory of aetiology in male homosexuality, 'International Journal of Psycho-analysis', 49, 27-37.

— (1969), The desire for sexual transformation: a psychiatric evaluation of transsexualism, 'American Journal of Psychiatry', 125, 1419-25.

— (1972), Homosexuality - basic concepts and psychodynamics, 'International Journal of Psychiatry', 10, 118-25.

Spensley, James and Barter, James T. (1971), The adolescent transvestite on a psychiatric service: family patterns, 'Archives of Sexual Behavior', 1, 347-56.

Spiegel, Rose (1960), Intensive psychotherapy of a nonhospitalized schizophrenic patient, 'American Journal of Orthopsychiatry', 30, 528-38.

Spitz, Rene A. (1945), Hospitalism, 'Psychoanalytic Study of the Child', 1, 53-74.

— (1946), Hospitalism: a follow-up report, 'Psychoanalytic Study of the Child', 2, 113-17.

— (1951), The psychogenic diseases in infancy, 'Psychoanalytic Study of the

Child', 6, 255-75.
— (1956), Transference: the analytical setting and its prototype, 'International Journal of Psycho-analysis', 37, 380-5.
Spitz, Rene A. and Wolf, Katherine M. (1946), Anaclitic depression, 'Psychoanalytic Study of the Child', 2, 313-42.
Spring, William J. (1939), Observations on world destruction fantasies, 'Psychoanalytic Quarterly', 8, 48-56.
Stabenau, James R. (1973), Schizophrenia: a family's projective identification, 'American Journal of Psychiatry', 130, 19-23.
Starer, Emanuel, Weinberger, Julius and Ahbel, Gertrude (1963), An analysis of polygraphic responses of chronic regressed male schizophrenic patients to Freudian-type stimuli, 'Journal of Clinical Psychology', 19, 43-4.
Stein, Lilli (1957), 'Social class' gradient in schizophrenia, 'British Journal of Preventive and Social Medicine', 11, 181-95.
Stevenson, I. and Wolpe, J. (1960), Recovery from sexual deviation through overcoming non-sexual neurotic responses, 'American Journal of Psychiatry', 116, 737-42.
Stokes, John H. (1940a), The personality factor in psychoneurogenous reactions of the skin, 'Archives of Dermatology and Syphilology, 42, 780-801.
— (1940b), A clinical analysis of pruritus ani, 'New International Clinics', 1, 147-58.
Stoller, Robert J. (1964a), A contribution to the study of gender identity, 'International Journal of Psycho-analysis', 45, 220-6.
— (1964b), Gender-role change in intersexed patients, 'Journal of the American Medical Association', 188, 684-5.
— (1964c), The hermaphroditic identity of hermaphrodites, 'Journal of Nervous and Mental Disease', 139, 453-7.
— (1967), Transvestites' women, 'American Journal of Psychiatry', 124, 333-9.
— (1968), 'Sex and gender', New York, Science House.
— (1969), A biased view of 'sex transformation' operations, 'Journal of Nervous and Mental Disease', 149, 312-17.
— (1971), The term 'transvestism', 'Archives of General Psychiatry', 24, 230-7.
— (1972), Etiological factors in female transsexualism: a first approximation, 'Archives of Sexual Behavior', 2, 47-64.
— (1973a), The impact of new advances in sex research on psychoanalytic theory, 'American Journal of Psychiatry', 130, 241-51.
— (1973b), Male transsexualism: uneasiness, 'American Journal of Psychiatry', 130, 536-9.
— (1974), 'Splitting: a case of female masculinity', London, Hogarth Press.
— (1975), 'The transsexual experiment', London, Hogarth Press.
Stoller, Robert J. and Newman, Lawrence E. (1971), 'The bisexual identity of transsexuals: two case examples, 'Archives of Sexual Behavior', 1, 17-28.
Stoller, R.J., Garfinkel, Harold and Rosen, Alexander C. (1960), Passing and the maintenance of sexual identification in an intersexed patient, 'Archives of General Psychiatry', 2, 379-84.
Stoller, Robert J., Marmor, J., Bieber, I., Gold, R., Socarides, C.W., Green, R. and Spitzer, R.L. (1973), A symposium: should homosexuality be in the APA nomenclature?, 'American Journal of Psychiatry', 130, 1207-16.
Storr, Anthony (1974, (first published 1964)), 'Sexual deviation', Harmondsworth, Penguin.
Stott, D.H. (1956), The effects of separation from the mother in early life, 'Lancet', 1, 624-8.
Sturup, Georg K. (1960), Sex offenses: the Scandinavian experience, 'Law and Contemporary Problems', 25, 361-75.
Suttie, Ian D. (1935), 'The origins of love and hate'. London, Kegan Paul, Trench, Trubner & Co.
Swanson, David W., Loomis, S. Dale, Lukesh, Robert, Cronin, Robert and Smith, Jackson A. (1972), Clinical features of the female homosexual patient, 'Journal of Nervous and Mental Disease', 155, 119-124.
Swartzburg, Marshall, Schwartz, Arthur H., Lieb, Julian and Slaby, Andrew E.

(1972), Dual suicide in homosexuals, 'Journal of Nervous and Mental Disease, 155, 125-30.

Swersie, Allan K. (1960), Six decades of inadequacy in a pseudohermaphrodite, 'Journal of Urology', 84, 771-2.

Swyer, G.I.M. (1954), Homosexuality: the endocrinological aspects, 'Practitioner', 172, 374-7.

Szasz, Thomas S. (1972), 'The myth of mental illness', St Albans, Granada.

— (1973), 'The manufacture of madness', St Albans, Granada.

Szurek, S.A. and Berlin, I.N. (1956), Elements of psychotherapeutics with the schizophrenic child and his parents, 'Psychiatry', 19, 1-9.

Tapia, Fernando (1960), Schizophrenogenic mothers, 'Diseases of the Nervous System', 21, 47-9.

Tauber, Edward S. (1940), Effects of castration upon the sexuality of the adult male, 'Psychosomatic Medicine', 2, 74-87.

Tausk, Victor (1934), Ibsen the Druggist, 'Psychoanalytic Quarterly', 3, 137-41.

Taylor, A.J.W. and McLachlan, D.G. (1962), Clinical and psychological observations on transvestism, 'New Zealand Medical Journal', 61, 496-506.

— (1963), Further observations and comments on transvestism, 'New Zealand Medical Journal', 62, 527-9.

— (1964), Transvestism and psychosexual identification, 'New Zealand Medical Journal', 63, 369-72.

Taylor, Helen W. and Humphrey, Edwin J. (1962), Congenital anomalies and chromatin sex reversal, 'American Journal of Obstetrics and Gynaecology', 84, 491-2.

Thompson, Clara (1947), Changing concepts of homosexuality in psychoanalysis, 'Psychiatry', 10, 183-9.

Thompson, Janet (1951), Transvestism: an empirical study, 'International Journal of Sexology', 4, 216-19.

Thorner, H.A. (1949), Notes on a case of male homosexuality, 'International Journal of Psycho-analysis', 30, 31-5.

Tolentino, I. (1957), Transvestitismo e transessualismo. Considerazioni sugli aspetti nosografico, eziopatogenetico e clinico di un caso di autocastrazione in un transessuale, 'Rivista Sperimentale di Freniatria', 81, 909-40.

Torrey, E. Fuller (1973), Is schizophrenia universal? An open question, 'Schizophrenia Bulletin', 7, 53-9.

Turtle, Georgina (1963), 'Over the sex border', London, Gollancz.

Van Krevelen, D. Arn (1960), Autismus infantum, 'Acta Paedopsychiatrica', 27, 97-107.

— (1971), Early infantile autism and autistic psychopathy, 'Journal of Autism and Childhood Schizophrenia', 1, 82-6.

Van Krevelen, D. Arn and Kuipers, Christine (1962), The psychopathology of autistic psychopathy, 'Acta Paedopsychiatrica', 29, 22-31.

Vogt, J.H. (1968), Five cases of transsexualism in females, 'Acta Psychiatrica Scandinavica', 44, 62-88.

Waelder, Robert (1951), The structure of paranoid ideas, 'International Journal of Psycho-analysis', 32, 167-77.

Walinder, Jan (1967), 'Transsexualism', Goteborg, Scandinavian University Books.

— (1968), Transsexualism: definition, prevalence and sex distribution, 'Acta Psychiatrica Scandinavica, Supplementum', 203, 255-7.

— (1971), Incidence and sex ratio of transsexualism in Sweden, 'British Journal of Psychiatry', 119, 195-6.

Ward, Ingeborg L. and Renz, Francis J. (1972), Consequences of perinatal hormone manipulation on the adult sexual behavior of female rats, 'Journal of Comparative and Physiological Psychology', 78, 349-55.

Ward, Jack L. (1958), Homosexual behavior in the institutionalized delinquent, 'Psychiatric Quarterly, Supplement', 32, 301-14.

Wardle, C.J. (1961), Two generations of broken homes in the genesis of conduct and behaviour disorders in childhood, 'British Medical Journal', 2, 349-54.

Weakland, John H. and Fry, William F. (1962), Letters of mothers of schizo-

phrenics, 'American Journal of Orthopsychiatry', 32, 604-23.
Weinberg, George (1975), 'Society and the healthy homosexual'. Gerrards Cross, Bucks, Colin Smythe.
West, D.J. (1974), 'Homosexuality', Harmondsworth, Penguin.
— (1977), 'Homosexuality Re-examined'. London, Duckworth.
Wheeler, Stanton (1960), Sex offenses: a sociological critique, 'Law and Contemporary Problems', 25, 258-78.
White, Robert B. (1961), The mother-conflict in Schreber's psychosis, 'International Journal of Psycho-analysis', 42, 55-73.
— (1963), The Schreber case reconsidered in the light of psychosocial concepts, 'International Journal of Psycho-analysis', 44, 213-21.
Wiedeman, George H. (1953), Transvestism, 'Journal of the American Medical Association', 152, 1167.
— (1962), Survey of psychoanalytic literature on overt male homosexuality, 'Journal of the American Psychoanalytic Association', 10, 386-409.
— (1964), Some remarks on the aetiology of homosexuality, 'International Journal of Psycho-analysis', 45, 214-16.
Williams, J.E. Hall (1960), Sex offenses: the British experience, 'Law and Contemporary Problems', 25, 334-60.
Williams, Jessie M. (1961), Children who break down in foster homes: a psychological study of patterns of personality growth in grossly deprived children, 'Journal of Child Psychology and Psychiatry', 2, 5-20.
Wilmer, Harry A. (1958), Toward a definition of the therapeutic community, 'American Journal of Psychiatry', 114, 824-34.
Winnicott, D.W. (1956), On transference, 'International Journal of Psycho-analysis', 37, 386-8.
— (1965), 'The maturational processes and the facilitating environment'. London, Hogarth Press.
Winterstein, Alfred (1956), On the oral basis of a case of male homosexuality, 'International Journal of Psycho-analysis', 37, 298-302.
Wittkower, Eric (1950), Psychiatry and the skin, 'Proceedings of the Royal Society of Medicine', 43, 799-801.
Wolf, Sanford R., Knorr, Norman J., Hoopes, John E. and Meyer, Eugene (1968), Psychiatric aspects of transsexual surgery management, 'Journal of Nervous and Mental Disease', 147, 525-31.
Wolfenden, Sir John et al. (1957), 'Report of the Committee on Homosexual Offences and Prostitution', London, HMSO.
Wolfenden, Sir John (1968), Evolution of British attitudes toward homosexuality, 'American Journal of Psychiatry', 125, 792-7.
Wolff, Charlotte (1971), 'Love between women', London, Duckworth.
— (1977), 'Bisexuality', London, Quartet Books.
Woods, Sherwyn M. (1972), Violence: psychotherapy of pseudohomosexual panic, 'Archives of General Psychiatry', 27, 255-8.
Woodward, Mary (1958), The diagnosis and treatment of homosexual offenders, 'British Journal of Delinquency', 9, 44-59.
Worden, F.G. and Marsh, J.T. (1955), Psychological factors in men seeking sex transformation: a preliminary report, 'Journal of the American Medical Association', 157, 1292-8.
World Health Organization (1962), 'Deprivation of maternal care', Geneva, WHO.
Wulff, M. (1942), A case of male homosexuality, 'International Journal of Psycho-analysis', 23, 112-20.
Wynne, Lyman C., Ryckoff, Irving M., Day, Juliana and Hirsch, Stanley I. (1958), Pseudo-mutuality in the family relations of schizophrenics, 'Psychiatry', 21, 205-20.
Wynne, Lyman C. and Singer, Margaret Thaler (1963a), Thought disorder and family relations of schizophrenics: a research strategy, 'Archives of General Psychiatry', 9, 191-8.
— (1963b), Thought disorder and family relations of schizophrenics: a classification of forms of thinking, 'Archives of General Psychiatry', 9, 199-206.
Zetzel, Elizabeth R. (1956), Current concepts of transference, 'International

Journal of Psycho-analysis', 37, 369-76.

Zilboorg, Gregory (1944), Masculine and feminine: some biological and cultural aspects, 'Psychiatry', 7, 257-96.

— (1956), The problem of ambulatory schizophrenias, 'American Journal of Psychiatry', 113, 519-25.

Zuger, Bernard (1966), Effeminate behavior present in boys from early childhood: the clinical syndrome and follow-up studies, 'Journal of Pediatrics', 69, 1098-1107.

Zuk, Gerald H. and Boszormenyi-Nagy, Ivan (eds) (1967), 'Family therapy and disturbed families', Palo Alto, California, Science and Behavior Books.

NAME INDEX

something the matter with our
ideas of reference

Homosexuality is a problem
of gender identity

Rather than sexuality as in
gender reassignment

Body image

Radical disidentification

The continuing capacity for
identification

the non conflictual
imperative of feminine

A close symbiosis with the
father mother, absent father

It is not the closeness to
the mother

of homosexuality not difference
in relation to the opposite sex

Blocking of the fulfilment
of identificatory love need

Transsexual = cross gender
identity
Same sex disidentification
& ambivalence

absence of same sex identity

P. 34
P. 35

A defensive detachment
is the negative of an unful-
-filled love need
H.s not an overtly sexual phe

Defensive: antimasculinity
Defensive detachment on the fath
fixation to the other not
abnormal
latent in overt authority probler
Boy's gender identity =
a masculine σ identification
fulfilling of gender identity
Homosexuality is not constitutive
authority problem or a ut the
opposite sex

pre-oedipal undifferentiate
phase) mother child, but
Homosexuality not a drive
but a defense mechanism